DAVID C. COOK
Discipleship Junction

And The Winner Is...

Sheila Seifert

NEXGEN®

Building the New Generation of Believers

COOK COMMUNICATIONS MINISTRIES
Colorado Springs, Colorado • Paris, Ontario
KINGSWAY COMMUNICATIONS LTD
Eastbourne, England

NexGen® is an imprint of
Cook Communications Ministries
Colorado Springs, CO 80918
Cook Communications, Paris, Ontario
Kingsway Communications, Eastbourne, England

AND THE WINNER IS...
© 2007 by Cook Communications Ministries

Cover Design: BMB Design
Cover Illustration: BMB Design/Ryan Putnam
Interior Design: TrueBlue Design/Sandy Flewelling
Interior Illustrations: Aline Heiser

First Printing 2007
Printed in the United States of America

1 2 3 4 5 6 7 8 9 10 Printing/Year 11 10 09 08 07

ISBN 978-0-7814-4512-2   105279

Table of Contents

WELCOME TO DISCIPLESHIP JUNCTION!

Discipleship Junction is an all-new program that harnesses the power of *FUN* to build young disciples through interaction with Bible truth and with each other.

A complete, multi-age children's ministry program, *Discipleship Junction* is packed full of interactive stories and drama, Scripture memory, and themed snacks and activities that will engage every child! It is guaranteed effective because its principles and methods of instruction are *teacher-tested* and *kid-approved!*

Intensive student-teacher interaction within a learning community that is relational and supportive makes *Discipleship Junction* an ideal program for including children with disabilities. Hands-on learning activities are easily adapted to include all students. For more ideas about inclusion, an excellent resource is *Let All the Children Come to Me* by MaLesa Breeding Ed.D., Dana Hood, Ph.D., and Jerry Whitworth, Ed.D., (Colorado Springs: Cook Communication Ministries, 2006).

PUTTING THE PIECES TOGETHER

Get Set. We know you're busy, so we provide a list of materials and what you'll need to prepare for your lesson. You'll also need a photocopy machine and some basic classroom supplies: paper, pencils, markers, butcher paper, scissors, glue, and index cards. When you see this icon  allow a little extra prep time.

Kids love to dress up! Many of our Bible lessons use costume props from the *Bible time dress-up box*. This can be as simple as a box of items you gather from around the house or purchase inexpensively from a second-hand store. It should include: fake beards, swords, headcloths and browbands, bath robes, modern day dress-ups, crown, decorative chains and belts, etc.

Tickets Please! *(10 minutes)* Each week begins with an activity option to involve children while others are being dropped off by parents.

■ The *Welcome Time Activity* will excite children's interest and help them connect with the Bible Truth for the week.

All Aboard for Bible Truth! *(20 minutes)* Whole group, interactive Bible lessons invite students ages 6–11 to participate in the entire lesson. Whether it's role-playing Zaccheus or running a feather relay, kids will be engaged in exciting, hands-on lessons.

■ Pre- and post-lesson discussion times encourage children to talk about their own life experiences and tie their knowledge to the week's Bible Truth.

■ *Use the Clues!* Practice is an important part of learning, and helps us move information from short-term to long-term memory. *And the Winner Is...* uses the exciting theme of running a race—complete with a winner's jersey and ribbons—to help children practice and apply what they have learned. At the end of every lesson you'll pin an illustrated winner's ribbon onto a class "winner's jersey." In the weeks that follow, students are repeatedly challenged to remember the Bible Truths connected with the ribbon illustrations. These "memory hooks" help the Bible Truth stick with kids for a long time to come.

Bible Memory Waypoint *(5 minutes)*. Toe tappin' and finger snappin'... there's nothing like the power of FUN to motivate children. Movement, rhythm, and role-play make it easy for kids to hide God's Word in their hearts (Psalm 119:11).

Prayer Station (15 minutes). Small-group prayer time for children. Wow! What an idea! Children break into small groups of three to five with an adult helper—we call them StationMasters. Using reproducible instruction cards, adults guide children to explore and practice new prayer skills. Together they'll share concerns, praise God, and practice the four activities of prayer: *praise, ask, confess, give thanks.*

(Optional) **Snack Stop and Activities** (10 minutes). Tied to the theme of the lesson, you have options for snacks and activities in which lesson truths are practiced and shared. Look for the throttle icon which shows the level of mess, energy or noise required for the activity!

On the Fast Track! Reproducible take-home pages invite families to interact in and through fun activities and Bible memory.

■ Are you looking for an additional way to motivate young learners? *Discipleship Junction* includes an optional incentive program which rewards students for completing take-home pages. Children return a signed *Fast Track!* Ticket and choose a prize from the treasure box. If you have a new student, you might welcome that child with the choice of a treasure too! Simply cover and decorate a large shoebox. Fill with inexpensive items such as you might find at a party store.

HOW TO GET STARTED

1. **Begin by recruiting StationMasters**—adult helpers who will guide children through the process of praying in small groups. Don't have enough adult volunteers? How about recruiting middle- or high-schoolers to shepherd a group? Also consider enlisting a few faithful prayer partners who will commit to praying for your class weekly.

■ Plan to have a brief training session with your volunteers in which you'll explain how to use the imPACT model of prayer . Each week you'll give the StationMasters a reproducible instruction card with the day's prayer theme and prayer suggestions to use with children in a small group.

2. **Set up your room.** You'll need a big area for your large-group Bible teaching time. You'll also need to identify spaces for each of your small prayer groups. Don't forget that moving chairs and tables or moving groups to a hallway is always an option. And children are willing helpers!

3. **Photocopy reproducible letters** (see Resources) to StationMasters and parents. Mail these two or three weeks before you begin your children's ministry program.

4. **Photocopy On the Fast Track!** pages for each child, and *StationMaster Cards* for each adult helper. If you choose, make copies of the reproducibles for all the lessons ahead of time. This can save a last-minute scramble when time is tight!

5. **Prepare the winner's jersey and ribbons.** Get an inexpensive size XXL t-shirt in a solid, bright color and mount it to the wall in your teaching area. Make copies of the winners' ribbons (see Resources). Then, add some color, number them on the back according to their corresponding lessons, and cut them out. Finally, fold a 14" length of 2" wide satin ribbon in half and staple it to the back of each medallion. Each week during *Use the Clues!* time, you'll pin one ribbon to the t-shirt. You can ask for volunteers to name the Bible Truth associated with each ribbon.

6. **Gather and prepare your materials,** set out your snacks, and you are ready to roll. So ... **FULL SPEED AHEAD! ALL ABOARD FOR DISCIPLESHIP JUNCTION!**

Memory Verse:

I consider everything a loss compared to the surpassing greatness of knowing Christ Jesus my Lord, for whose sake I have lost all things. I consider them rubbish, that I may gain Christ **(Philippians 3:8).**

*Early elementary verse in **bold** type.*

Bible Basis:
1 Corinthians 9:23–26

Bible Truth:
Winners choose to give their best in the race of life.

Give Your Best!

You Will Need:

- [ ] winner's jersey mounted on a wall
- [ ] ribbon #1
- [ ] 1 poster board
- [ ] simple games (pick-up sticks, jacks, etc.)
- [ ] feathers or ping-pong balls
- [ ] 8½" x 11" cardboard pieces
- [ ] Bibles
- [ ] masking tape
- [ ] *On the Fast Track! #1* take-home paper
- [ ] *StationMaster Card #1*
- [ ] (optional) treasure box
- [ ] (optional) snack: granola bars or trail mix, fruit punch or sports drink, cups
- [ ] (optional) Activity #1: paper, paper fasteners, markers or crayons, scissors
- [ ] (optional) Activity #2: balloons, beanbags, ping-pong balls

When you see this icon, it means preparation will take more than five minutes.

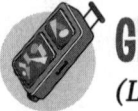

GET SET!
(Lesson Preparation)

- ■ Print today's Bible memory verse on a poster board:
  I consider everything a loss compared to the surpassing greatness of knowing Christ Jesus my Lord, for whose sake I have lost all things. I consider them rubbish, that I may gain Christ (Philippians 3:8).
- ■ Make a copy of *On the Fast Track! #1* take-home paper for each child.
- ■ Make a copy of *StationMaster Card #1* for each helper.
- ■ Make masking tape starting and finish lines in the main classroom area.
- ■ Create a sample jointed self-portrait figure using the instructions in Activity #1 if using that option.
- ■ Set out the winner's jersey for *Use the Clues!* and (optional) treasure box.
- ■ Set up snack and outside play activities if you include these items in your children's ministry.

TICKETS PLEASE!
(Welcome and Bible Connection)

- ■ *Objective: To excite children's interest and connect their own life experiences with the Bible Truth, children will play simple games to experience winning and losing.*

Welcome Time Activity: Games to Win

■ *Materials: jacks and ball, pick-up sticks, and/or other simple games*
Set the games you have on the tables and invite children to find one or more partners and play. They can also play "Rock, Paper, Scissors" and simple guessing games like "I Spy" and "Twenty Questions."

Sharing Time and Bible Connection

■ *Materials: feathers or ping-pong balls, 8½" x 11" cardboard pieces*

When everyone has arrived, call children to the lesson area and welcome them. As you move into the activity and discussion to prepare for the Bible story, give every child the opportunity to say something.

Did you all have fun playing those games? Ask the children whether they won or lost their games and how that made them feel. **We would all rather win than lose, wouldn't we?**

Now we're going to play a game that requires some teamwork.

Ask children to pair up and stand in a line shoulder to shoulder. Give each pair a feather or ball, and each player a cardboard piece. Tell them that, as partners, they need to move their feather/ball across the room to a designated spot without touching it with their hands. Tell partners they have 30 seconds to make a plan. Then say "go" and let them play until everyone finishes.

When all are seated again, discuss the game.

■ **What did it take for you to be able to finish that race?** (working together, effort, keeping your mind on the race, listening to your partner, keeping your eyes on the goal, sticking to your plan, not giving up)

■ **If you've been in other kinds of races, what was important to be able to finish the race?** (endurance, training, discipline, practice, listening to the coach, knowing the rules, doing your best)

■ **How is everyday life as a follower of Jesus like being a runner in a race?** (you need many of the same qualities, you can't give up, you do your best, you follow Jesus)

■ **Is winning all that counts in a race?** (no, how you run is more important than winning)

Many people think the only thing that counts in a race is winning. God doesn't think that way. He wants most of all for you to run your best. He wants you to be a winner in your attitude and your spirit. Today and for the next twelve weeks, we are going to figure out how to be winners in God's kingdom.

Today we're going to discover what Paul, a great leader of Christians in Bible times, said about running in the race of life.

ALL ABOARD FOR BIBLE TRUTH

(Bible Discover and Learn Time)

1 Corinthians 9:23–26

■ **Objective:** *Children will study 1 Corinthians 9:23–26 to learn how Paul compared life to a race and what it takes to be a winner in God's kingdom.*

■ **Materials:** *Bibles, masking tape starting and finish lines*

How do we know what is great in God's kingdom? Accept children's responses. Point to the starting line on one side of the classroom. **To be a winner, first you have to get into the race.** Point to the finish line on the other side of the classroom. **And then you have to know how to reach the finish line. We're going to read what the apostle Paul said about life and racing.** Divide the class into small groups of four to six children, with confident readers or helpers in each group. Pass out Bibles to those who need them and have each child find 1 Corinthians 9:23–26. Have confident readers in each group read the verses aloud.

What did Paul write about being in a race? Accept children's responses. **He said that life is like a race.** Have children all line up at the starting line. **In a race, Paul said all the runners run to try to be the first one across the finish line.** Let children run to the finish line. Those who are unable to run can walk or use other means. Adapt this activity so everyone in your class can move from the starting to ending point.

Did Paul tell us everyone would win the race? No, he said even though all the runners train and run their best, only one will win. Paul said that people should live life as if they were in a race and wanted to win.

Paul gives us some great hints for how to be a winner in life. What's one of them? Pause for responses. **He says we need to exercise self-control. What do you think of when you hear the word self-control?** Accept student responses. **Being self-controlled means we discipline ourselves to do the right things everyday—even when it's hard. We get up on time in the morning, do our work at school and home to the best of our ability, try not to make sinful choices, and obey our parents even when we don't feel like it.**

What would happen if all the runners in a race wanted to run in different directions? (it wouldn't be fair, runners might crash into each other, etc.) **Runners who want to win all run in the same direction, to the same finish line. A winner in God's kingdom runs the way God says, not any old way that's easy or feels good.**

Good runners work hard so they have a chance of being the winner. What are some ways you can think of to be a winner in the race of life? (praying, encouraging others, being patient, kind, generous, etc.)

Paul lived his life so he could learn to know God better. He used self-control so everything he did would be pleasing to God.

Like Paul, if we learn to run the race of life well, we'll be winners. Winning the race of life and being a winner in God's kingdom isn't about being the fastest or strongest. It's about how we

live and how we follow Jesus. <u>Giving our best to Jesus means we'll be great in God's kingdom</u>. Over the next twelve weeks, we'll find out how to be winners from other Bible time people too.

Use the Clues!
(Bible Review)

- **Materials:** *masking tape starting and finish lines*

Okay, let's see what you remember.

Show the children the winner's jersey and explain that each week, the class will add a new winner's ribbon to the jersey. The symbol on the award will help them remember what they learned from the Bible that week.

Divide the class into two teams and have the teams each select one representative "runner." Direct the runners to stand behind the masking tape starting line. As you ask each review question, watch for the team member who raises his hand first. If that child answers the question correctly, then his runner can take a giant step toward the finish line. If the child doesn't answer correctly, give the other team a chance to answer. Feel free to keep the race relatively even by asking the other team for alternative answers.

- **How did Paul say we should run the race of life?** (run to win)

- **What are some qualities Paul said we need to win the race of life?** (self-control, discipline)
- **What are some ways we can be self-controlled?** (do the right things, obey even when we don't feel like it, try hard all the time)
- **What race should we all aim to win?** (the race of life to be a winner in God's kingdom)
- **Do we all have to have strong bodies and be fast on our feet to be winners in God's kingdom?** (no, we win by the way we live and the way we follow Jesus)

Choose a child from the winning team to pin ribbon #1 on the winner's jersey. Remind children on the losing team that, although they didn't win this particular race, they can be winners in God's kingdom every day by following Jesus and loving others. Ask the child with the ribbon to identify the symbol (pair of running shoes) and how it's a reminder of this week's Bible story (life is a race we run to be winners in God's kingdom).

BIBLE MEMORY WAYPOINT
(Scripture Memory)

Philippians 3:8

- **Objective:** *Children will hide God's Word in their hearts for guidance, protection, and encouragement.*

I consider everything a loss compared to the surpassing greatness of knowing Christ Jesus my Lord, for whose sake I have lost all things. I consider them rubbish, that I may gain Christ (Philippians 3:8).

To help children memorize today's verse, read it aloud from the poster, and then read it with the children as you point to the words. Use this game to further practice the verse. Have children line up on one side of the room. **We're going to have a slow motion race. You can take a step when we all say a word from the memory verse.** Say the memory verse with your students. The first time through, you should say a word and have your students repeat it. When they repeat it, they can take a step forward. The goal is to reach the other side of the room as quickly as possible. Continue repeating the memory verse until students are able to walk quickly to the other side of the room.

PRAYER STATION

- **Objective:** *Children will explore and practice prayer for themselves in small groups.*
- **Materials:** *Copies of StationMaster Card #1 for each adult or teen helper*

Break into small groups of three to five children. Assign a teen or adult helper to each small group and give each helper a copy of *StationMaster Card #1* (see Resources) with ideas for group discussion and prayer.

SNACK STOP: HIGH ENERGY RACE SNACKS (Optional)

If you plan to provide a snack, this is an ideal time to serve it.

- **Materials:** *granola bars or trail mix, fruit punch or sports drink, cups*

Have you ever seen a real running race? When it's a long race, people on the sidelines will hand runners a drink as they run past to keep them from getting too hot and tired. This snack is a good one for keeping your energy up. What other kinds of food give you lots of energy? Discuss with the children that reading the Bible and learning it is spiritual food to keep us running in the race of life for God. Let children tell you some verses they've memorized as they finish their snack.

Note: Always be aware of children with food allergies and have another option on hand if necessary.

APPLICATION

■ *Objective: Children will have opportunities to show how the lesson works in their own lives through activities and take-home papers.*

Some children's ministries may allow children to play outside at this point. If yours does not, choose one of the following activities.

Runner Figures

■ *Materials: paper, paper fasteners, markers or crayons, scissors*

Show children your sample jointed self-portrait figure. They should draw themselves on the paper, taking up as much of the sheet as possible (a small drawing is harder to cut out and successfully join with paper fasteners). Once they've drawn themselves, show how to cut it out so that the legs and arms are separate pieces, then joined to the trunk with paper fasteners. After they've made the figures, have them play "Winner Says" with them (adapt the same rules as "Simon Says" for this game).

Relay Races

■ *Materials: balloons, beanbags, ping-pong balls*

Depending on the physical abilities of children in your class, plan some relay races like passing a balloon down the line, balloon volleyball, a beanbag toss where team members toss the bag back and forth to each other a certain number of times, or blowing a ping-pong ball across a table top. Choose games that allow everyone in the class to play, even if they have a physical limitation.

ON THE FAST TRACK! *(Take-Home Papers)*

Introduce the treasure box: **Who would like to choose a prize from the treasure box?** Expect excited responses. **Today I'm going to give each of you an *On the Fast Track!* paper to take home. When you've done the activities and memorized the Bible verse, ask a parent or guardian to sign the ticket** (show ticket). **When you bring this back next week, you'll get to have a turn at the treasure box.**

Distribute the take-home papers and jointed figures, if made, just before children leave.

LESSON TWO: Under Authority

Memory Verse:

And we know that **in all things God works for the good of those who love him,** who have been called according to his purpose **(Romans 8:28).**

*Early elementary verse in **bold** type.*

Bible Basis:

Esther 4:1—5:2

Bible Truth:

Winners say yes to God's authority.

You Will Need:

- [ ] winner's jersey mounted on a wall
- [ ] ribbon #2
- [ ] 1 poster board
- [ ] magnets
- [ ] cardboard tube or drumstick
- [ ] Bible time dress-up box
- [ ] 2 crowns *(optional)*
- [ ] soccer or kick ball
- [ ] *On the Fast Track! #2* take-home paper
- [ ] *StationMaster Card #2*
- [ ] *(optional)* treasure box
- [ ] *(optional)* snack: fruit chunks (pineapple, apple, orange, grapes, melon), wooden skewers
- [ ] *(optional)* Activity #1: cardboard tube
- [ ] *(optional)* Activity #2: fun foam sheets, glue, markers or colored pencils, glitter, magnets, scissors *(optional)*

 ***When you see this icon, it means preparation will take more than five minutes.***

 ## GET SET!
(Lesson Preparation)

- ■ Print today's Bible memory verse on a poster board: **And we know that in all things God works for the good of those who love him, who have been called according to his purpose (Romans 8:28).**
- ■ Make a copy of *On the Fast Track #2* take-home paper for each child.
- ■ Make a copy of *StationMaster Card #2* for each helper.
- ■ 🕐 Cut out a 3" x 3" fun foam square for each child if using Activity #2.
- ■ Set out the winner's jersey for *Use the Clues!* and *(optional)* treasure box.
- ■ Set up snack and outside play activities if you include these items in your children's ministry.

 ## TICKETS PLEASE!
(Welcome and Bible Connection)

- ■ ***Objective:*** *To excite children's interest and connect their own life experiences with the Bible Truth, children will play a game about being under an authority.*

Welcome Time Activity: Submit to the Scepter

■ *Materials:* *wand or stick, such as a cardboard tube, drumstick, etc.*
As children arrive, invite them to join the game. Players will take turns being the king or queen and using the scepter to command the other players to complete actions. For example, the king/queen will command, "hop around the room on one foot," and point the scepter at the other players. The players continue the action until the king/queen lowers the scepter. They freeze until a new command is issued and the scepter is again lifted. Change royalty often and encourage kids to be creative with their commands.

Sharing Time and Bible Connection
■ *Materials:* *magnets for every pair of students, pencils, paper*

When everyone has arrived, call children to the lesson area and welcome them. As you move into discussion to prepare for the Bible story, give every child the opportunity to say something.

Explain to the children that you are going to pair them up and give each pair some "authority." **When something has authority, it means that other things should obey it, right?** Pass out the magnets and ask the children to go around the room and find as many objects that will "obey the magnet's authority" as they can. Have them keep a list of the objects they try (some will be magnetic, some shouldn't be). Give them a few minutes for this activity.

Then, gather the children together for discussion.

■ **What kinds of objects did you find that "obeyed" or stuck to your magnets? What objects didn't?**
■ **How are you and I sometimes like the non-magnetic objects?** (we don't obey those in authority over us)
■ **When are we like magnetic objects?** (when we do respond to and obey the authority over us)
■ **Who are people in authority over us?** (parents, teachers, pastors, government leaders)

Being winners in our spiritual lives means we must understand that we're under authority. God is our top authority—he's in charge of us. And he's made other people to be in charge of us too. A lady in the Old Testament found out how important it was to be under someone's authority. Let's see what happened.

ALL ABOARD FOR BIBLE TRUTH!
(Bible Discover and Learn Time)

Esther 4:1–5:2

- ■ **Objective:** *Children will study Esther 4 and 5 and discover how Esther obeyed God and paid her respect to a king in authority over her.*
- ■ **Materials:** *chair, cardboard tube, Bible time dress-up box, 2 crowns (optional)*

What do you think it's like to be a queen? Let children offer their thoughts.

Back in the early times of the Bible, in the land of Persia, the king chose a queen because of her youth and beauty. But the queen didn't get to rule the land. Only the king was in charge. He decided who got to live and who would be put in prison or killed. To see the king was a special privilege.

The book of Esther tells an amazing story of a Jewish woman who became the queen of Persia. The Jews, God's chosen people, had many enemies in that land so Esther had a special role to play to protect her people.

Choose children to act out parts of the king, Esther, messenger, two guards, and a Persian subject. After they choose dress-up clothes from the box, put crowns on the king and Esther. The king also will have the cardboard tube scepter.

Place the king on the chair in the middle of the class, with the guards on either side of the throne. Have children sit a distance from him. Position Esther in a different place where the children can see her well. Direct actors to silently act out the story as you tell it.

Esther's cousin was named Mordecai. Mordecai found out that an evil man who worked for the king had made up a wicked plan. Mordecai sent a messenger to tell Esther the news.

"Esther, there's danger! Mordecai sent me to tell you that Haman, the king's top official, cooked up a plan to kill all the Jews. He hates our people."

Esther was full of fear for her people. "What can I do?" she asked the messenger.

He said, "You should go to the king and ask him to help save our people."

Now Esther was really scared. "I can't just go see the king," she said. "There's a law that says anyone who goes in to see the king without being invited will be put to death. That means I could die for going to see him without an invitation. Only if the king holds out his golden scepter to people can they be saved from death."

The messenger told Mordecai what Esther said, and back he came with another message. "Queen Esther, Mordecai says that the Jews may not be saved any other way but by your asking the king for help."

Esther realized she had to do this. She asked every Jew in the area to fast and pray with her for three days. After that, Esther said, "I will go to the king, even though it is against the law. And if I die, I die."

So what do you think happened?

After three days of asking God for courage and for the king to answer her request, Esther put on her royal robes. She walked to the king's inner courtyard. The king looked out and saw Queen Esther. And he was glad to see her! He held out his golden scepter, so she was able to go to him and ask for his help to save the Jews. The king had the evil man, Haman, put to death and even helped the Jews protect themselves from more of their enemies.

Because Esther <u>obeyed God and gave respect to the king in authority over her</u>, she was able to keep her people from being killed. As we saw in this story, kings have a lot of authority. The Bible describes God as the King of kings. He has authority over everyone and everything, including human kings, queens, presidents, and governments. Now, that's a lot of authority!

Use the Clues!
(Bible Review)

■ *Materials:* soccer or kick ball

Let's do a little review of the Bible story.

To make the review into a game, have the children stand in a wide circle. They should kick the ball gently around the circle, everyone getting a chance to kick it. After a few kicks, say stop. Whoever the ball goes to next will try to answer a review question. If they succeed, have the group give loud cheers and claps, then start kicking the ball gently around the circle again.

■ **Who was the person in authority in Persia during the time of Queen Esther?** (the king)
■ **What problem did Esther have?** (she heard about a plan to kill her people, the Jews, and needed to ask the king to stop the plan; she hadn't been invited to see the king and might have been killed for going in to him)
■ **What made Esther a winner in God's kingdom?** (she obeyed God and protected His chosen people while also respecting the king's authority over her)
■ **Who else did Esther respect as an authority over her?** (her cousin Mordecai)
■ **Who is in authority over us and is worthy of our respect and obedience?** (God, teachers, parents, grandparents, law officers, pastors, etc.)

Have a child pin ribbon #2 on the winner's jersey. Ask the child to identify the symbol (scepter) and how it's a reminder of this week's Bible story (the king used the scepter to accept a visitor).

Review last week's lesson by asking a child what the running shoes on ribbon #1 stand for.

BIBLE MEMORY WAYPOINT
(Scripture Memory)

Romans 8:28

■ *Objective: Children will hide God's Word in their hearts for guidance, protection, and encouragement.*
■ *Materials: cardboard tube scepter*

And we know that in all things God works for the good of those who love him, who have been called according to his purpose (Romans 8:28).

To help children memorize today's verse, read it aloud from the board, then read it with the children as you point to the words. Repeat the verse a couple of times together. Practice the verse by choosing a child to be the king or queen. The child will walk around the group and hold the scepter over someone who should say as much of the verse as possible. Then the class should finish the verse in unison. After a couple of repeats, choose a new person to hold the scepter. Aim for children to say more and more of the verse each time.

Note: be sensitive to shyer students and consider having the king or queen only point the scepter toward volunteering children.

 # PRAYER STATION

- **Objective:** *Children will explore and practice prayer for themselves in small groups.*
- **Materials:** *Copies of* StationMaster Card #2 *for each adult or teen helper*

Break into small groups of three to five children. Assign a teen or adult helper to each small group and give each helper a copy of *StationMaster Card #2* (see Resources) with ideas for group discussion and prayer.

 # SNACK STOP: FRUIT SCEPTER (Optional)

If you plan to provide a snack, this is an ideal time to serve it.

- **Materials:** *fruit chunks (pineapple, apple, orange, grapes, melon), wooden skewers*

You can either make the scepters ahead of time or have bowls/plates of fruit for the children to thread on their skewer. Talk about manners for meeting royalty, such as curtseying and bowing, and waiting until the royalty eats first to take a bite of food. Let children share their ideas about royalty and living in a palace.

Note: Always be aware of children with food allergies and have another option on hand if necessary.

APPLICATION

■ *Objective: Children will have opportunities to show how the lesson works in their own lives through activities and take-home papers.*

Some children's ministries may allow children to play outside at this point. If yours does not, choose one of the following activities.

 ### The King's Invitation

■ *Materials: cardboard tube*

Have one volunteer act as queen or king, sit in a chair and hold the tube. Choose two guards who stand near the king. Everyone else will try to reach the king, who will touch them with the scepter. Meanwhile, the guards will try to tag those coming to the king/queen. Those tagged become guards and tag others. Play until all are either tagged or safe, then choose a new queen/king and guards and play again.

When the game is over, explain that the king's rules apply to everyone, so everyone must obey them. Remind children that God is our king.

 ### Under God's Authority Magnets

■ *Materials: 3"x 3"fun foam squares or fun foam sheets in a variety of colors, glue, markers or colored pencils, glitter, magnets, scissors (optional)*

If you have not cut out the fun foam squares, have children do so. Then allow them to draw, color, add other fun foam shapes, and/or glitter the squares with something that will remind them that they are under God's authority (e.g., an umbrella, a tree, a crown, or words like, "God Rules," "King of kings," "Under God," etc.). Lastly, have students glue their squares to the magnets and allow to dry.

Discuss what it means to be under God's authority: to obey God and those he puts over us like parents and teachers, to be respectful in attitude, words, and actions toward God and other authorities.

 ### ON THE FAST TRACK! *(Take-Home Papers)*

Let children who brought back a signed ticket from last week's take-home paper choose a prize from the treasure box. **Today I'm going to give every child an *On the Fast Track!* paper to take home. To earn a prize, complete all the activities this week and learn the verse that's on the page. When you're finished, ask a parent or guardian to sign the ticket. Bring it with you next week and you'll get to choose a prize from the treasure box!**

Distribute the take-home papers and magnets, if made, just before children leave.

LESSON THREE: Act Like a Winner

Memory Verse:
Even a child is known by his actions, by whether his conduct is pure and right (Proverbs 20:11).

Bible Basis:
Daniel 6

Bible Truth:
Winners act like winners in all they do.

You Will Need:

- [ ] winner's jersey mounted on a wall
- [ ] ribbon #3
- [ ] 1 poster board
- [ ] small building blocks
- [ ] 5 toy people
- [ ] box or bag of small stones
- [ ] stuffed or toy lions
- [ ] *On the Fast Track! #3* take-home paper
- [ ] *StationMaster Card #3*
- [ ] (optional) treasure box
- [ ] (optional) snack: round crackers or cookies, whipped cream cheese or frosting, raisins, chocolate chips, plastic knives, coarsely grated carrot or thin licorice strands cut in 1" pieces
- [ ] (optional) Activity #2: beads of various types (including those suitable for boys), beading twine, scissors

When you see this icon, it means preparation will take more than five minutes.

GET SET!
(Lesson Preparation)

- Print today's Bible memory verse on a poster board:
  Even a child is known by his actions, by whether his conduct is pure and right (Proverbs 20:11).
-  For the Welcome Time Activity, write out actions on paper slips. Actions can be acting mad, acting happy, acting like a monkey, acting like a baby, acting silly, acting shy, acting hungry, etc.
- Photocopy *On the Fast Track! #3* take-home paper for each child.
- Photocopy *StationMaster Card #3* for each helper.
- Set out the winner's jersey and (optional) treasure box.
- Set up snack and outside play activities if you include these items in your children's ministry.

TICKETS PLEASE!
(Welcome and Bible Connection)

- *Objective: To excite children's interest and connect their own life experiences with the Bible Truth, children will play charades to show different ways of acting.*

Welcome Time Activity: Charades

■ *Materials: slips of paper with different actions*
As children arrive, direct them to where a couple of helpers are playing charades. Children will take turns choosing a slip of paper. A helper can whisper what it says if the child can't read or understand it. Then the child will act out what's on the paper. Helpers will prompt the others to guess the action by asking, "What is he/she acting like?"

Sharing Time and Bible Connection

When everyone has arrived, call children to the lesson area and welcome them. Introduce the lesson with a discussion, using the following questions. As you talk, give every child the opportunity to say something.

Many times you can tell something about a person by the way they act.

■ **What would you think of a person who acts silly all the time?**
■ **How about someone who acts like they know everything?**
■ **Think of people who win. What do they act like?** Ask children to use their bodies and facial expressions to show you how winners might act.
■ **Do you think all winners act like this?**
■ **What kinds of things can you win besides a game or sport?** (being a winner in God's kingdom)
■ **So how does a winner in God's kingdom act?** (submits to authority, self-controlled, disciplined, does his best)

That's what we're going to discover today. Many Bible people are examples to us of being winners in God's kingdom. One of them was a man who was taken away from his own city and made to live in a different country. Let's see how he acted like a winner.

ALL ABOARD FOR BIBLE TRUTH   Daniel 6
(Bible Discover and Learn Time)

■ *Objective: Children will study Daniel 6 to learn how Daniel's actions showed he was a winner because he refused to honor anyone above God.*
■ *Materials: small building blocks, stuffed or toy lions, small stones, 5 toy people*

Before we find out what the Bible says about our winner, we need to build a few things. Ask several children to construct a house with a window using wooden or plastic building blocks. Ask another group to make a foot-wide circle with stones.

Have the group sit down and choose some children to act out the story with the toy figures as you tell it. You will need a Daniel, a king, three officials, and some lions.

Our winner lived in Israel, but he was taken away as a teenager to live in a different country called Babylon. His name was Daniel (have the child with the Daniel figure act like he's being captured), **and many other Jews were taken away too. Daniel trusted in the one true God, even when the people in his new country didn't know or follow God. Because Daniel was honest and lived by God's truth, God gave him wisdom and courage. The king in this new country trusted him so much that he was going to put Daniel in charge of the whole kingdom** (have Daniel bow to the king and the king come close to him). **How do you think that made the other officials feel?** (angry, jealous, frustrated) **They were mad and jealous that a foreigner could have so much power. These men didn't like that Daniel was honest and a hard worker. They didn't like that he was wise and faithful to the one true God. They wanted to make Daniel look bad so the king wouldn't like him, but they couldn't find anything that Daniel did wrong! So they made up a plan** (have officials huddle together, scheming).

They persuaded King Darius to make a law that no one could pray to any god or man except him for 30 days. That sounded like a great idea to the king. Then the officials said, "If anyone disobeys, they should be thrown into the lion's den." King Darius signed the law.

Daniel knew he could get into a lot of trouble from this law because he prayed to God every day. But Daniel was a winner in God's kingdom. He wasn't about to pray to anyone but God (have Daniel go inside the house, visible through the window). **Three times every day he went into his house and knelt down by his window. He prayed and praised God. Daniel didn't change his actions; he wasn't going to stop being a winner in God's kingdom.**

The officials were just waiting to catch Daniel praying. As soon as they saw him praying, they ran to King Darius (have officials go to the king). **"O great Darius. Remember your law? Guess what? Daniel is praying to his God!"**

King Darius was so upset! He didn't want to punish Daniel. But the officials wouldn't let him make an exception to the law. So the king ordered Daniel to be dropped into a pit of hungry lions.

Have children with the lions put them in the ring of rocks and act hungry. **King**

Darius said to Daniel, "May your God, who you faithfully serve, save you!"

That night, the king was too upset to eat, and he couldn't sleep. As soon as the sun came up the next morning, King Darius threw on his king's robes and raced to the lion pit (have the king run to the ring of rocks). **He called down into the hole, "Daniel, servant of the living God, has your God been able to save you from the lions?"**

Do you think he was expecting a voice? Daniel called back, "O King, my God sent his angel to shut the lions' mouths so they wouldn't hurt me. God knows I didn't do anything wrong."

Whew! The king was so relieved. He commanded Daniel to be taken out of the lion's pit. Because <u>Daniel had acted like a winner for God,</u> the

king and all his people heard about God's power and faithfulness (have Daniel act like he just won).

Use the Clues!
(Bible Review)

Let's talk a bit about the Bible story!

- **What made the king of Babylon trust Daniel?** (he was honest, hard working, faithful to God, and wise)
- **Why did Daniel get in trouble?** (he prayed to God when there was a law that said people should pray only to the king)
- **How did Daniel act like a winner?** (he chose to do what was right in God's eyes even when it wasn't right to other people, he was faithful to God no matter what happened)

- **What happened because Daniel was a winner for God's kingdom?** (God saved him from being eaten by lions and caused the king to honor God too)

Have a child pin ribbon #3 on the winner's jersey. Ask the child to identify the symbol (silhouette of figure through a window) and how it's a reminder of this week's Bible story (Daniel would not pray to anyone but the true God).

Review previous lessons by letting children call out what the symbols on the other ribbons stand for.

BIBLE MEMORY WAYPOINT
(Scripture Memory)

Proverbs 20:11

- **Objective:** *Children will hide God's Word in their hearts for guidance, protection, and encouragement.*
- **Materials:** *stuffed or toy lion*

Even a child is known by his actions, by whether his conduct is pure and right (Proverbs 20:11).

To help children memorize today's verse, read it aloud from the board, then read it with the children as you point to the words. Repeat the verse a couple of times together. To practice the verse some more, have the children line up in two lines, facing each other. If you have a large class, make two sets of two lines. Each set of lines will need a toy lion. Toss the lion to the first person in one line. They'll say the first word of the verse. Then that child tosses it to the child across from him, who repeats the first word and says the next word of the verse before tossing the lion to the second child in the line facing her. In this way, the toy is tossed back and forth, moving down the line, as the verse grows word by word. You can repeat this activity by having everyone say the words in unison while the lion is passed. Play until the verse is implanted in children's memories.

PRAYER STATION

- ■ **Objective:** *Children will explore and practice prayer for themselves in small groups.*
- ■ **Materials:** *Copies of* StationMaster Card #3 *for each adult or teen helper*

Break into small groups of three to five children. Assign a teen or adult helper to each small group and give each helper a copy of *StationMaster Card #3* (see Resources) with ideas for group discussion and prayer.

SNACK STOP: LION MANES (Optional)

If you plan to provide a snack, this is an ideal time to serve it.

- ■ **Materials:** *round crackers or cookies, whipped cream cheese or frosting, raisins, chocolate chips, plastic knives, coarsely grated carrot or thin licorice strands cut in 1" pieces*

Remember the lions from the Bible story? It would be really strange to see a lion acting like a rabbit, wouldn't it? We can tell a lion by the way it acts. Let's make some lions to eat. Children can spread cream cheese or frosting on the crackers or cookies and make a face with raisins or chocolate chips, then add a mane by pushing carrot shreds or licorice strips around the cookie like a mane. While children enjoy their snacks, remind them that you can recognize winners by how they act.

Note: Always be aware of children with food allergies and have another option on hand if necessary.

APPLICATION

- ■ **Objective:** *Children will have opportunities to show how the lesson works in their own lives through activities and take-home papers.*

Some children's ministries may allow children to play outside at this point. If yours does not, choose one of the following activities.

Action Mimics

Children will produce actions consistent with a certain person or creature. Choose three or more types of animal or occupation for each round. Work with helpers to whisper one of the ideas to each child, making sure there are at least two of each animal or occupation. Once everyone has received a whispered instruction of what to act like, tell the class to start. They should begin acting and sounding like whatever they were told. Children should find others who are acting out the same thing and make a pair with them. When everyone has a partner, ask children to name what they were acting like. Explain that just like snakes or carpenters or kings act a certain way, winners in God's kingdom also act a certain way. People can see if they are a winner with God by how they act. Play again with new animals, occupations, or helping roles.

Animals: snake, elephant, horse, chicken, fish, kangaroo, bee, etc.

Occupations: carpenter, cook, truck driver, photographer, dancer, gardener, house builder, etc.

Reminder Jewelry

- **Materials:** *beads of various types (including those suitable for boys), beading twine, scissors*

Children will string beads to make a piece of jewelry—ring, bracelet, anklet, or choker necklace. Tell them that every time they put their creation on, they can be reminded to act like a winner in all they do. Helpers can assist children to tie knots, string beads and fasten jewelry pieces.

ON THE FAST TRACK! *(Take-Home Papers)*

Let children who brought back a signed ticket from last week's take-home paper choose a prize from the treasure box. **When you take your *On the Fast Track!* paper home each week and do the activities, your parents can sign the ticket that you finished the work. You can bring the signed ticket back and get a prize from the treasure box.**

Distribute the take-home papers and jewelry, if made, just before children leave.

LESSON FOUR: All Ears

Pay Attention!

Memory Verse:

My sheep listen to my voice;
I know them, and they follow me
(John 10:27).

Bible Basis:

1 Samuel 3:1–20

Bible Truth:

Winners pay attention
to God's voice.

You Will Need:

- [ ] winner's jersey
- [ ] ribbon #4
- [ ] 1 poster board
- [ ] noisemakers (bell, toy animals that make noises, hammer and wood, small bouncing ball, musical instrument, drinking glass, spoon)
- [ ] 4 squares of different colored paper
- [ ] earmuffs or earplugs
- [ ] nightlight *(optional)*
- [ ] tape or CD
- [ ] cassette or CD player
- [ ] Bibles
- [ ] floor mats or blankets
- [ ] balloons
- [ ] 1 or 2 permanent markers
- [ ] *On the Fast Track! #4* take-home paper
- [ ] *StationMaster Card #4*
- [ ] *(optional)* treasure box
- [ ] *(optional)* snack: graham crackers, peanut butter, plastic knives
- [ ] *(optional)* Activity #1: 2–4 playground balls, masking tape
- [ ] *(optional)* Activity #2: paper, markers, stickers, a variety of round objects

GET SET!
(Lesson Preparation)

- ■ Print today's Bible memory verse on a poster board: **My sheep listen to my voice; I know them, and they follow me (John 10:27).**
- ■ Photocopy *On the Fast Track! #4* take-home paper for each child.
- ■ Photocopy *StationMaster Card #4* for each helper.
- ■ Plan to dim or turn off the room lights for the Bible story. If you think your children would be disturbed by darkness, prepare to leave a door open a bit or use a nightlight. If the room has much natural light, make arrangements to reduce it.
- ■ Make a tape or CD recording of a voice (preferably a man's) for use in the Bible story. Separate each segment by 5 seconds of silence. Segment #1: "Samuel, Samuel." #2: "Samuel." #3: "Samuel." #4 "Samuel, Samuel." #5: "I am about to do something in Israel that will make the ears of anyone who hears of it tingle. I'm going to do what I said I would do to Eli. I told him that I will punish him and his family for all the sin they have done."
- ■ Inflate and tie 14 balloons of one color for small classes, or two groups of 14 balloons (each group a different color) for large classes.
- ■ Set out the winner's jersey for *Use the Clues!* and *(optional)* treasure box.
- ■ Set up snack and outside play activities if you include these items in your children's ministry.

When you see this icon, it means preparation will take more than five minutes.

TICKETS PLEASE!
(Welcome and Bible Connection)

■ **Objective:** *To excite children's interest and connect their own life experiences with the Bible Truth, children will try to identify sounds.*

Welcome Time Activity: Name that Sound

■ **Materials:** *noisemakers (bell, toy animals that make noises, hammer and wood, small bouncing ball, musical instrument, drinking glass, spoon)*

Children should cover their eyes while a helper uses the noisemakers to make sounds, one at a time, for children to identify. After all the sounds are identified, ask the children to make other sounds so others can guess what they are.

Sharing Time and Bible Connection

■ **Materials:** *4 squares of different colored papers, earmuffs or earplugs*

When everyone has arrived, call children to the lesson area and welcome them. As you move into the activity and discussion to prepare for the Bible story, give every child the opportunity to say something.

Recruit three volunteers. Have two put on earmuffs or earplugs. Give each child a set of four different colors of paper and have them face away from you. Explain that you will tell them what order to put their papers in. Each time they get it right, they get a point. Do the experiment three to four times, then total their points.

■ **Who do you think won the game?** (the one with no hearing obstruction)
■ **Why did that one do the best at the game?** (because he/she could listen well to the teacher's voice)
■ **When you play other games, what sounds do you need to pay attention to?** (coach's voice, whistle, other players)
■ **How often would you win at a game if you didn't pay attention to what was happening?** (never, not often)

Playing a game is just one example of when you need to pay attention. In school, at home, when you're crossing the street, and when you're growing in your life with God are other times. Today you'll see how one boy paid attention when other people weren't, and why he was a winner.

📖 ALL ABOARD FOR BIBLE TRUTH
(Bible Discover and Learn Time)

1 Samuel 3:1-20

- ■ **Objective:** *Children will learn from 1 Samuel 3:1–20 how Samuel paid attention to God and grew up as a winner in God's kingdom.*
- ■ **Materials:** *Bibles, floor mats or blankets, voice recording, tape or CD player, nightlight (optional)*

The person in our story today was a boy, maybe even the same age as some of you. He was living in the temple to learn how to be a priest of the Lord. His teacher was an old man, a priest named Eli. But Eli and his sons didn't pay attention to God. They did many things that dishonored Him, and God was preparing to get rid of them. God knew who would take Eli's place. This boy Samuel was God's choice.

Divide children into two groups and assign one group to be Samuels and the other group to be Elis. As you tell the story, have the children act out their assigned parts.

Samuel wasn't sure what it meant to listen and pay attention to God, but he wanted to learn how. One night he was sleeping in his little room in the temple. Eli was asleep in his own room. Dim or turn off the lights. Have the children lie on blankets or floor mats on the floor and pretend to sleep. Play recording #1. **Samuel woke up and ran down to Eli's room.** Have each Samuel run to an Eli. **He said to Eli, "Here I am, you called me." But Eli said, "I didn't call you. Go back to bed." Samuel was surprised, but he did what Eli said.** Have the Samuels go back to their "rooms" and lie down. Play recording #2. **Samuel heard the voice and again he ran to Eli. "Here I am!" he said, "You called me." "No, I didn't call you, my son. Go back to bed." Samuel didn't know what was going on, but he obeyed Eli. And not long after he lay down again, he heard it again.** Play recording #3. **After Samuel went to Eli's room again, Eli finally understood that God was calling. Eli told Samuel, "Go lie down, and if God calls you again, say, 'Speak Lord, for your servant is listening.'" So Samuel went back and lay down.**

And soon he heard the Lord calling him. Play recording #4. **Samuel paid attention and answered. This time Samuel said:** Prompt children to say, "Speak Lord, for your servant is listening." **Then the Lord talked to him.** Play recording #5. Have all of the children sit up and face you as you finish the story.

How do you think Samuel felt? The Bible says he stayed in his bed until morning, and was afraid to tell Eli what God had said. But Eli wanted to know, so Samuel told him. And God did what he promised with Eli's family. When Samuel grew up, God made him a prophet in Israel. He was an important leader because he listened and paid attention to whatever God said.

Would you say Samuel was a winner? Yes, he did his best and followed God in every way. He's a great example to us of <u>paying attention to God's voice</u> and becoming a winner in God's kingdom.

Use the Clues!
(Bible Review)

■ **Materials:** *balloon(s)*

I'm going to see what you remember!
Let the children scatter throughout the room. Blow up a balloon and then release it to fly around the room. The child to whom it's closest will try to answer the question. Repeat with the balloon for the next question. You may need to use a fresh balloon after a couple of uses, depending on the type of balloon.

■ **Who was Samuel?** (a boy who was learning how to serve God as a priest in the temple)
■ **How did Samuel pay attention to God?** (he listened and responded whenever he heard God's voice)
■ **What was the difference between Samuel and Eli and his sons?** (Samuel was a winner because he listened to God and did what God wanted, but Eli and his sons sinned and didn't pay attention to God's voice)
■ **How did Samuel become a winner in God's kingdom?** (by being careful to listen, by knowing God's voice and answering, by following God faithfully all his life)
■ **How can you and I be winners like Samuel?** (pay attention to God's voice so we can answer when he speaks, do our best in our lives with God)
■ **Samuel actually heard God's voice. What are some other ways that we can listen to God?** (listening for his voice in people around us, reading the Bible, paying attention to ideas we have to help others)

Have a child pin ribbon #4 on the winner's jersey. Ask the child to identify the symbol (an ear) and how it's a reminder of this week's Bible story (Samuel paid attention to God's voice).

Review past weeks' lessons by pointing to ribbons and having children name the stories and what the stories say about being a winner for God's kingdom.

BIBLE MEMORY WAYPOINT   John 10:27
(Scripture Memory)

■ **Objective:** *Children will hide God's Word in their hearts for guidance, protection, and encouragement.*
■ **Materials:** *inflated balloons (different colors for different teams), permanent markers*

My sheep listen to my voice; I know them, and they follow me (John 10:27).

To help children memorize today's verse, read it aloud from the poster board, then read it with the children as you point to the words. Use this game to further practice the verse. Divide into two teams (small classes can do this as a single group). Have helpers work with teams to write one word of the verse on each balloon. Then play a game where teams bat their balloons in the air until you give the signal. Then they collect their team's balloons and reconstruct the verse in correct order.

 **PRAYER STATION**

- ■ **Objective:** *Children will explore and practice prayer for themselves in small groups.*
- ■ **Materials:** *Copies of* StationMaster Card #4 *for each adult or teen helper*

Break into small groups of three to five children. Assign a teen or adult helper to each small group and give each helper a copy of *StationMaster Card #4* (see Resources) with ideas for group discussion and prayer.

 **SNACK STOP: SNACKS AT ATTENTION** **(Optional)**

If you plan to provide a snack, this is an ideal time to serve it.

- ■ **Materials:** *graham crackers, peanut butter, plastic knives*

Distribute graham crackers to each child and tell them they'll need to pay attention to you in order to eat their snack. **If you're paying attention, you'll feel me touch your back. Then you can eat your snack.** Ask children to pretend they're sleeping, like Samuel, by putting their heads on the table and closing their eyes. You'll walk silently around the room and touch children gently on the back. Pass the peanut butter and knives to spread on their crackers if they choose.

Note: Always be aware of children with food allergies and have another option on hand if necessary.

 **APPLICATION**

- *Objective:* Children will have opportunities to show how the lesson works in their own lives through activities and take-home papers.

Some children's ministries may allow children to play outside at this point. If yours does not, choose one of the following activities.

 **Dodge Ball**

- *Materials:* 2–4 playground balls, masking tape

Make a tape line in the center of the playing area. Divide into two teams, with teams facing each other on opposite sides of the line. Give each side one or more balls. The object is to toss the ball to get someone on the other team out. Only hits that land below the belly button count. When a player is touched by a ball, that child sits on the sidelines until the game is over. Remind children they have to pay attention where the balls are so they won't be hit. Children who can't run or move quickly can be referees to let children know when they've been hit and are out. Reinforce how paying attention can make you a winner in this game, just like paying attention to God's voice makes you a winner in His kingdom.

 **Target Practice**

- *Materials:* paper, markers, stickers, a variety of round objects

Have children create a target by tracing four round objects, each one inside the other and successively smaller. As they color in the rings, discuss how they might hear God this week (prompting to obey, ideas on how to serve others, etc.). Explain that they'll take their target home and post it. Each day they can add a sticker to a ring if they've paid attention to God by reading Scripture, praying, and doing what's right. They'll add a sticker to the outer ring the first day, the next ring the second day, until they reach the center. Challenge them to do their best to pay attention to God this week.

 **ON THE FAST TRACK!** *(Take-Home Papers)*

Who would like to choose a prize from the treasure box? Allow students who brought back their signed tickets to choose a prize. **Here's your next** *On the Fast Track!* **paper. Make sure you complete all of the activities and memorize your Bible verse. Then have a parent or guardian sign it and bring it with you next week. If you do, you'll get to choose a prize from the treasure box!**

Distribute the take-home papers and targets, if made, just before children leave.

LESSON FIVE: True Trust

Memory Verse:

Trust in the LORD with all your heart and lean not on your own understanding; in all your ways acknowledge him, **and he will make your paths straight (Proverbs 3:5–6).**

*Early elementary verse in **bold** type.*

Bible Basis:

2 Kings 6:8–23

Bible Truth:

Winners trust God.

You Will Need:

- [ ] winner's jersey
- [ ] ribbon #5
- [ ] 1 poster board
- [ ] blindfold
- [ ] small object (stapler, crown, etc.)
- [ ] large resealable bag
- [ ] wooden skewer
- [ ] bucket
- [ ] Bible time dress-up box
- [ ] colored slips of paper
- [ ] *On the Fast Track! #5* take-home paper
- [ ] *StationMaster Card #5*
- [ ] (optional) treasure box
- [ ] (optional) snack: split bagels or mini bagels, cream cheese, candy sprinkles, bear-shaped graham crackers, plastic knives
- [ ] (optional) Activity #1: cardboard tubes cut to 2" lengths or card stock in 2"-wide strips, 8½"-long construction paper strips, yarn, stapler, tape, scissors

When you see this icon, it means preparation will take more than five minutes.

GET SET!
(Lesson Preparation)

- Print today's Bible memory verse on a poster board: **Trust in the Lord with all your heart and lean not on your own understanding; in all your ways acknowledge him, and he will make your paths straight (Proverbs 3:5–6).**
- Photocopy *On the Fast Track! #5* take-home paper for each child.
- Photocopy *StationMaster Card #5* for each helper.
- Make four photocopies of the Bible story and highlight one speaking part on each script. The four parts are King of Aram, officer, Elisha, and servant.
- Fill a large re-sealable bag with water.
- Cut colored paper into slips for the memory verse practice.
- Set out the winner's jersey for *Use the Clues*! and (optional) treasure box.
- Set up snack and outside play activities if you include these items in your children's ministry.

TICKETS PLEASE!
(Welcome and Bible Connection)

- ***Objective:*** *To excite children's interest and connect their own life experiences with the Bible Truth, children will play Blind Hunt to start them thinking about trust*

Welcome Time Activity: Blind Hunt

■ *Materials: blindfold, a small object (stapler, crown, etc.)*
Have children form a large circle. Choose one child to be "it" and blindfold her.
Spin her around several times while another child places a small object somewhere
in the circle. "It" tries to find the object using the directions the other players give
her. When she finds the object, she may choose another player to be "it."

*Note: to make this game more challenging, hide the object somewhere in the room
and limit the words the other children can say, i.e., hot or cold.*

Sharing Time and Bible Connection

■ *Materials: large resealable bag filled with water, wooden skewer, bucket*

When everyone has arrived, call children to the lesson area and welcome
them. As you move into the activity and discussion to prepare for the
Bible story, give every child the opportunity to say something.
**Have any of you ever been in a scary situation that ended up
being all right?** Prompt children to think about a roller coaster ride or a
time they were lost and then their mom found them. **Today I'm going
to try an experiment that could be a little scary. May I have a volunteer?** Pull your large bag of water out of the bucket and hold it over your
volunteer's head. Hold the sharp end of the skewer close to the bag. **I am going to poke
the skewer into this bag. Do you trust me?** Look at the rest of the group. **Do you all
think [volunteer's name] should trust me?** Push the skewer all the way through the
bag at its fattest part where there are no wrinkles. No water should leak out. Have everyone applaud the volunteer, and allow him or her to take a seat.

**Today we're going to discover what one of God's winners, Elisha, found out
when he was in a scary situation.**

ALL ABOARD FOR BIBLE TRUTH   2 Kings 6:8–23
(Bible Discover and Learn Time)

■ *Objective: Children will discover from 2 Kings 6:8–23 how Elisha learned to trust God even
when surrounded by enemies.*
■ *Materials: Bible time dress-up box, highlighted Bible story copies*

Select four good readers, and hand each a highlighted photocopy. Let each volunteer
choose an appropriate item from the Bible dress-up box to wear while they read their

parts. Readers should then stand at the front of the class. You'll read the narration parts, with the children reading their parts at appropriate times.

Narrator: **One of God's prophets in Bible times was Elisha** (point to Elisha reader). **He took over as a prophet in Israel when God took Elijah to heaven. Elisha showed us in this situation what it means to trust God no matter what.**

    Israel was at war with the country of Aram. The king of Aram would plan with his officers where to camp before attacking the Israelites. But the Israelites kept finding out the king's secret plans! Oh, this made the king mad!

King Aram : (frowns) **This really bugs me. Who in my army is telling the Israelites my plans?**

Officer: **No one, my king. Elisha, the prophet in Israel, is the one who tells their king what you're saying.**

Narrator: **Elisha knew the king's plan because God told him what would happen.**

King Aram: (angrily) **Go and find where Elisha is. I'm going to capture him.**

Officer: **Elisha is in the town of Dothan.**

King Aram: **Aha!**

Narrator: **The king sent a huge company of horses and chariots to Dothan. He was going to be sure to capture Elisha. The chariots and horses arrived at Dothan at night and surrounded the whole city. They knew no one would escape, especially not Elisha! When Elisha's servant got up the next morning, he saw lots and lots of chariots and horses surrounding them. He went running to find Elisha.**

    Servant: (out of breath and very scared) **Help, help! Elisha, have you seen what's outside? We're surrounded!**

    Elisha: **Don't be afraid! There are more with us than with the enemy's army.**

    Servant: **What do you mean?**

    Elisha (praying): **O Lord, please open my servant's eyes so he can see.**

    Narrator: **What do you think the servant saw?** Let children respond, but don't give away the finale. **The servant already had his eyes open. But God gave him spiritual vision, and suddenly he saw what Elisha meant.**

Servant: **Wow! This is unbelievable! I see horses and chariots of fire all around us! The mountain is full of them!**

Narrator: **When the Aram army came down to capture Elisha, he prayed again.**

Elisha: **Lord, make these soldiers blind.**

Narrator: **God did! Not one of them could see. Then Elisha went out and told them they were in the wrong place. He led them to Samaria, Israel's capital. God let them see again, and they were frightened that they would be killed. But Elisha said no.**

Elisha: **Give them food and water. Then let them go back to their king.**

Narrator: **The soldiers took off back to Aram and told their king what happened. And they never raided Israel again.**

Thank the readers. **Sometimes things look pretty bad. They sure looked bad for Elisha and the Israelites! But, as this story shows us, God is bigger than our enemies and bigger than any situation we could ever be in. Just like I asked [earlier volunteer's name] to trust me with a bag of water over [his/her] head, <u>God asks us to trust him in every situation</u>. No matter what things seem like, God has everything under control. <u>And we can be winners like Elisha when we choose to trust God</u>!**

Use the Clues!
(Bible Review)

Let's do a little review of the Bible story we just heard. Listen closely to the questions and raise your hand if you know the answer.

- **Why was the king of Aram mad?** (God told Elisha what the king planned and Elisha told Israel's king about the enemy's plans)
- **Why was Elisha's servant scared?** (he could see the enemy's horses and chariots surrounding them)
- **Why wasn't Elisha scared?** (he knew God was in control of the situation and had put his own horses and chariots of fire)
- **What can we learn from Elisha's example?** (to trust God no matter what)
- **Does trusting God mean that we always get what we want?** (no, but it does mean that we recognize that God is in control and has a bigger picture in mind)

Have a child pin ribbon #5 on the winner's jersey. Ask the child to identify the symbol (flaming chariot) and how it's a reminder of this week's Bible story (even when Elisha was surrounded by the enemy, he trusted that God had things under control).

BIBLE MEMORY WAYPOINT   Proverbs 3:5–6
(Scripture Memory)

- ■ **Objective:** *Children will hide God's Word in their hearts for guidance, protection, and encouragement.*
- ■ **Materials:** *colored slips of paper*

Trust in the LORD with all your heart and lean not on your own understanding; in all your ways acknowledge him, and he will make your paths straight (Proverbs 3:5–6).

To help children memorize today's verse, read it aloud from the board, then read it with the children as you point to the words. Repeat the verse together a few times, then give half the children small slips of colored paper. Let everyone mix and mingle for a minute. Ask children holding a slip to find someone without a slip. The child with the paper will say the first half of the verse, then give the slip to his partner who will say the rest of the verse plus reference. The second child keeps the paper as the process is repeated. Do this several times until the verse is familiar.

PRAYER STATION

- ■ **Objective:** *Children will explore and practice prayer for themselves in small groups.*
- ■ **Materials:** *copies of* StationMaster Card #5 *for each adult or teen helper*

Break into small groups of three to five children. Assign a teen or adult helper to each group and give each helper a copy of *StationMaster Card #5* (see Resources) with ideas for group discussion and prayer.

SNACK STOP: BAGEL BLOCKADE (Optional)

If you plan to provide a snack, this is an ideal time to serve it.

- ■ **Materials:** *split bagels or mini bagels, cream cheese, candy sprinkles, bear-shaped graham crackers, plastic knives*

After children spread cream cheese on a bagel half, pass around the sprinkles and two bear-shaped graham crackers per child. They'll stick the bear-shaped graham crackers in the center of their bagels (Elisha and servant) and apply some sprinkles (the horses and chariots that surrounded them). As you eat, discuss how the children can trust God in their day-to-day lives.

Note: Always be aware of children with food allergies and have another option on hand if necessary.

 **APPLICATION**

■ **Objective:** *Children will have opportunities to show how the lesson works in their own lives through activities and take-home papers.*

Some children's ministries may allow children to play outside at this point. If yours does not, choose one of the following activities.

 ## Spiritual Binoculars

■ **Materials:** *cardboard tubes cut to 2" lengths or card stock in 2"-wide strips, 8½"-long construction paper strips, yarn, stapler, tape, scissors*

Children will construct "spiritual binoculars" to remind them to look at their situation with spiritual eyes and trust God. Children will lay two cardboard rolls on an 8 1/2"-long paper strip and secure the paper strip with tape. (If cardboard tubes aren't available, 2"-wide card stock strips can be rolled and taped or glued into short cylinders.) A length of yarn can be stapled to the tubes if desired so the binoculars can be worn around the neck. If you have time, have children share one way they will practice trusting God this week.

 ## Elisha Tag

Children line up at one end of the room, with two players—Elisha and his servant—in the center of the room. The goal is for the children to run from one end of the room to the other without being tagged by Elisha or his servant. Those who are tagged become taggers who must stand where they were tagged, but can reach out to touch runners. Elisha and the servant can move freely. The last two runners become the new Elisha and servant for the next game.

 ## ON THE FAST TRACK! *(Take-Home Papers)*

Let children who brought back a signed ticket from last week's take-home paper choose a prize from the treasure box. **I'm giving everyone an *On the Fast Track!* paper to take home. To earn a prize from the treasure box, complete all the activities at home and learn your verse. When you're finished, ask a parent or guardian to sign the ticket and bring it next week. If you do, you'll get to choose a prize!**

Distribute the take-home papers and spiritual binoculars, if made, just before children leave.

Talk to God!

Memory Verse:
Give thanks to the LORD, call on his name; make known among the nations what he has done (Psalm 105:1).

Bible Basis:
1 Samuel 1

Bible Truth:
Winners talk to God.

You Will Need:

- ☐ winner's jersey
- ☐ ribbon #6
- ☐ 1 poster board
- ☐ blindfold
- ☐ beanbag
- ☐ pretend or homemade megaphones
- ☐ construction paper
- ☐ *On the Fast Track! #6* take-home paper
- ☐ *StationMaster Card #6*
- ☐ *(optional)* treasure box
- ☐ *(optional)* snack: fresh flour tortillas or pita bread rounds
- ☐ *(optional)* Activity #1: paper, stapler, markers or colored pencils, colored paper
- ☐ *(optional)* Activity #2: masking tape, 2 empty soft drink bottles, 2 index cards

When you see this icon, it means preparation will take more than five minutes.

GET SET!
(Lesson Preparation)

- ■ Print today's Bible memory verse on a poster board: **O give thanks to the LORD, call on his name; make known among the nations what he has done (Psalm 105:1).**
- ■ Roll three or four sheets of paper into three or four megaphones.
- ■ Make two photocopies of the Bible story skit (see Resources).
- ■ Photocopy *On the Fast Track! #6* take-home paper for each child.
- ■ Photocopy *StationMaster Card #6* for each helper.
- ■ Set out the winner's jersey for *Use the Clues!* and *(optional)* treasure box
- ■ Set up snack and outside play activities if you include these items in your children's ministry.
- ■ Mark a starting line on one side of the room and two pairs of Xs on the other side with masking tape if using Activity #1.
- ■ ⌚ Write out instructions for Activity #1 on two index cards.

TICKETS PLEASE!
(Welcome and Bible Connection)

- ■ *Objective: To excite children's interest and connect their own life experiences with the Bible Truth, children will navigate a simple obstacle course while talking to the course coach.*

Welcome Time Activity: Obstacle Course

■ **Materials:** *blindfold*

As children arrive, have them join others going through an obstacle course, blindfolded. Set up chairs and tables to crawl under, walk around, and scoot past. A helper will act as a coach, but children will have to ask the coach for instructions. When unsure how to proceed, other players will call out, "talk to the coach."

Sharing Time and Bible Connection

When everyone has arrived, call children to the lesson area and welcome them. As you move into the activity and discussion to prepare for the Bible story, give every child the opportunity to say something.

Start by *silently* mouthing these words: **Have you ever talked to God without saying anything out loud?** As children look baffled, repeat the sentence silently.

■ **What do you think I was saying?** If anyone comes close to restating your silent speech, congratulate him or her.

I asked you if you have ever talked to God without saying anything out loud. But I could have been talking in a foreign language or just mouthing random words, couldn't I?

■ **Have you ever watched people move their mouths but not say any words? What did you think they were doing?**

There are lots of ways to talk to God. Ask for four volunteers to stand facing the class. Direct them to pretend to pray using the method you'll describe. Walk behind them and point at each one in turn as you mention each mode of prayer. **This person is praying out loud, like we do in class. This person is praying by singing. This person is praying silently, but not moving his mouth. This person is praying silently, but her mouth is moving like she's talking.**

Today we're going to investigate how a sad, hurting woman prayed. She's an example for us of how winners can talk to God.

ALL ABOARD FOR BIBLE TRUTH   1 Samuel 1
(Bible Discover and Learn Time)

■ **Objective:** *Children will study 1 Samuel 1 to find out how Hannah talked to God about her desire for a child.*

Use the skit in the Resources section to set the scene for this story. Invite two helpers or children to play the roles in the script.

In the skit, who was the coach? What did the player learn about talking to the coach? (a player needs to talk to the coach if he wants to do well in the game)

A few weeks ago we learned how a boy named Samuel paid attention to God's voice. Today we're looking at a lady named Hannah, who was Samuel's mother! But in our story today, Samuel wasn't born yet.

Hannah followed God and trusted in him. She was married to a man named Elkanah who also followed God. They were winners in God's kingdom because they trusted in him. But everything wasn't wonderful in their lives. Something huge was missing. Hannah had no children, and that was what she wanted most of all.

Think of something you've wanted so much you could hardly stand it. Let children share their thoughts. **So you know a little of how Hannah felt. There was nothing she could do to fix her problem, except one thing. She talked to God about it.**

Every year Elkanah and his household went to the Jewish temple at Shiloh to worship God and offer a special sacrifice. This was part of how they honored God. While Elkanah was making his sacrifices, Hannah went to the temple to talk to God. She was so upset and sad about having no children that she cried really hard.

"O Lord of hosts, if you will only be kind enough to me, your servant, to give me a son, I will dedicate him to serve you all his life," she prayed.

Hannah didn't know it, but someone was watching. She was praying in her heart and her mouth was moving, but she wasn't making any sounds. Say your first and last name or a sentence, but don't make any sound. Look at someone sitting near you while they do that. That's how Hannah would have looked.

The man who saw her was Eli, the priest of the temple, and he wondered what was wrong with this lady. He didn't realize she was talking to God about her sadness. Eli told Hannah to stop because he thought she was acting really strange. Hannah explained she was talking to God about her sorrow and Eli finally understood. Then he blessed her. "Go home with peace in your heart because God heard what you were saying to him."

Knowing that her prayers to God had been heard and would be answered changed Hannah. She was finally able to stop feeling so sad and lonely, and she

went home with a confident mind and heart. And before long, she was expecting her first baby to be born.

Hannah was a winner because she knew that talking to God was what would make the difference in her problem. She didn't whine at her husband or take out her frustration on others, or make excuses for herself.

Hannah showed us how to talk with God as we live our lives. That's what winners do. Remember the skit? The player was bummed out because he wouldn't get to play, so he couldn't win. All because he didn't talk to the coach. There's just no way to do our best in God's kingdom without talking to God. He knows exactly what it takes to win.

Use the Clues!
(Bible Review)

- *Materials: beanbag, 3 sheets each of 3 colors of construction paper*

Let's see what you remember.

Divide into two teams. Lay out 9 squares of paper: 3 each of 3 different colors, like a tic-tac-toe game. Assign point values to each color, for example red=10, blue=30, yellow=50.

Teams will alternate in tossing the beanbag onto a sheet of paper. If they answer a question right, they earn that number of points.

- **What was Hannah's problem?** (she wanted a baby, but couldn't have one)
- **What did Hannah do about her problem?** (prayed at the temple for God to give her a child)
- **Who heard Hannah's prayers?** (Eli the priest, God)
- **Why did the priest think Hannah was strange?** (because her lips were moving, but no sound was coming out)
- **How did Hannah come out a winner?** (she talked to God about her situation and trusted Him to help her)
- **Why do we sometimes not talk to God about things?** (we forget, we talk to other people instead, we think God doesn't care or can't help, we don't trust Him enough)

Congratulate the winning team. Let one child from that team pin ribbon #6 on the winner's jersey. Ask the child to identify the symbol (a baby) and how it's a reminder of this week's Bible story (Hannah talked to God and he heard her and gave her a child).

BIBLE MEMORY WAYPOINT   PSALM 105:1
(Scripture Memory)

- *Objective: Children will hide God's Word in their hearts for guidance, protection, and encouragement.*
- *Materials: pretend or homemade megaphones*

O give thanks to the Lord, call on his name; make known among the nations what he has done (Psalm 105:1).

To help children memorize today's verse, read it aloud from the board, then read it with the children as you point to the words. Ask a couple of older children to be your assistants as you use the megaphones to lead the rest of the class in practicing the verse in phrases like cheerleaders leading a cheer. Use rhythmic motions to accompany the words of each phrase as you shout them out, waiting for the children to imitate you before shouting the next phrase. After several repetitions, have everyone jump and cheer for their efforts.

PRAYER STATION

- **Objective:** *Children will explore and practice prayer for themselves in small groups.*
- **Materials:** *copies of* StationMaster Card #6 *for each adult or teen helper*

Break into small groups of three to five children. Assign a teen or adult helper to each small group and give each helper a copy of *StationMaster Card #6* (see Resources) with ideas for group discussion and prayer.

SNACK STOP: TORTILLA MEGAPHONES (Optional)

If you plan to provide a snack, this is an ideal time to serve it.

- **Materials:** *fresh flour tortillas or pita bread rounds*

Show children how to roll up their tortilla or pita into a funnel shape that functions as a megaphone. **Who can tell me what a megaphone does?** (they make talking sound louder so crowds can hear) **We don't have to worry about being loud enough for God. We can whisper, sing, or talk silently to Him and He hears us perfectly.**

Note: Always be aware of children with food allergies and have another option on hand if necessary.

APPLICATION

- **Objective:** *Children will have opportunities to show how the lesson works in their own lives through activities and take-home papers.*

Some children's ministries may allow children to play outside at this point. If yours does not, choose one of the following activities.

 **Prayer Notebook**

■ *Materials: paper, stapler, markers or colored pencils, colored paper*

Children will make small prayer notebooks. Cut 8 1/2" x 11" paper in half the short way. Show children how to fold the paper in half and make a cover with colored paper. Help them staple the books along the fold as a binding. Let them decorate their covers as they choose. Talk with them and ask their ideas on how to use these prayer notebooks this week. How will the notebook help them or remind them to talk to God? (they might write down what they've prayed about, how God answers, write down a prayer poem, etc.)

 **Coach Needed**

■ *Materials: masking tape, 2 empty soft drink bottles, 2 index cards*

Divide children into two teams, and choose one child from each team to be the "coach." Take the "coaches" aside and tell them how to play the game, but instruct them not to tell the others. (It may help if you have the instructions written out on an index card for each "coach.") To run the relay, children will take turns running to one of their team's two X marks and balancing the soft drink bottle upside down in the center of the X. They will then walk like a crab back to their team and tag the next team member. The second team member will run to the soft drink bottle, pick it up, move it and balance it on the second X, then return with the crab walk.

When you return to the rest of the group, say, **We're going to have a relay race. When I say, "go," you start. You may ask your coach for help on how to play, but you're only allowed to ask "yes" or "no" questions.** Give the coaches the empty soft drink bottles and say "go."

After a few rounds, call the children together and discuss the importance of being in constant communication with the person who has the big picture.

 ON THE FAST TRACK! *(Take-Home Papers)*

Who can explain how to get a prize from the treasure box? Let a volunteer explain how it works and then allow children who brought back a signed ticket from last week's take-home paper to choose their prizes. **That's right. When you do the activities and learn the verse on your *On the Fast Track!* paper this week, all you need to do is ask your parents or guardian to sign the ticket. When you bring it next week, you'll get to choose a prize from the treasure box!**

Distribute the take-home papers and prayer notebooks, if made, just before children leave.

LESSON SEVEN: Wisdom for Winners

Use Godly Wisdom!

Memory Verse:

If any of you lacks wisdom, he should ask God, who gives generously to all without finding fault, **and it will be given to him (James 1:5).**

*Early elementary verse in **bold** type.*

Bible Basis:

1 Samuel 25:2–35

Bible Truth:

Winners use God's wisdom to make the best choices.

You Will Need:

- [ ] winner's jersey
- [ ] ribbon #7
- [ ] 1 poster board
- [ ] magazines
- [ ] butcher paper or poster board
- [ ] piece of fruit
- [ ] handful of candy
- [ ] piece of bread
- [ ] Bible time dress-up box
- [ ] cardstock
- [ ] *On the Fast Track! #7* take-home paper
- [ ] *StationMaster Card #7*
- [ ] (optional) treasure box
- [ ] (optional) snack: loaf of bread, raisins, fig-bar cookies
- [ ] (optional) Activity #1: medium-sized baskets, bungee cords or strips of fabric, 6 or more empty food boxes or containers (such as oatmeal and cereal boxes, cookie tins, plastic peanut butter jars, etc.)
- [ ] (optional) Activity #2: cardstock or heavy-duty paper plates, paper fasteners, large paper clips, markers

When you see this icon, it means preparation will take more than five minutes.

GET SET!

(Lesson Preparation)

- ■ Print today's Bible memory verse on a poster board:

  If any of you lacks wisdom, he should ask God, who gives generously to all without finding fault, and it will be given to him (James 1:5).
- ■ Photocopy *On the Fast Track! #7* take-home paper for each child.
- ■ Photocopy *StationMaster Card #7* for each helper.
- ■ 🕐 Create a large jigsaw puzzle with pieces of cardstock, writing a couple of words from the memory verse on each sheet, then cut them to fit together as a floor puzzle. Hide the pieces around the room for later use.
- ■ Set out the winner's jersey for *Use the Clues!* and *(optional)* treasure box.
- ■ Set up snack and outside play activities if you include these items in your children's ministry.

TICKETS PLEASE!

(Welcome and Bible Connection)

- ■ **Objective:** *To excite children's interest and connect their own life experiences with the Bible Truth, children will play a game about choices.*

Welcome Time Activity: What to Choose?

■ *Materials:* *magazines, scissors, glue sticks, markers, butcher paper or poster board*
Ask early-arriving children to create a poster of images and ideas that represent making good choices. Choices may be related to friends, activities, entertainment, or food. They can cut out magazine images to collage on the butcher paper or poster board, or draw pictures. Casually engage children in conversation about what they've chosen and why.

Sharing Time and Bible Connection

■ *Materials:* *piece of fruit, handful of candy, piece of bread*

When everyone has arrived, call children to the lesson area and welcome them. As you move into the activity and discussion to prepare for the Bible story, give every child the opportunity to say something.

Ask a volunteer to come forward. Show them the food items and ask what they would choose if they could eat just one. After the volunteer chooses one, take a vote, asking the rest of the class who would make the same choice as the volunteer. Then ask who would choose each of the other two items. For each item, ask one child who voted for that item to share why they made that choice.

We make choices all the time. We choose what to eat, who to play with, whether to answer when our parents call us, and if we'll be a faithful friend or not. We make some choices just because we like certain things more than other things, like chocolate chip cookies instead of peanut butter cookies. But other choices we make, like whether to say mean things to someone or not, can be good and please God or bad and hurt God, yourself, and others.

■ **What are some other choices you make in a day?** (who to sit with at school, what to watch on TV or play on the computer, whether or not to finish homework, etc.)

God cares about the choices we make. And he is ready to give us a really important tool so we can make the best choices. Winners in God's kingdom use this tool to make good choices. In our Bible story, you'll find out what that tool is.

ALL ABOARD FOR BIBLE TRUTH

(Bible Discover and Learn Time)

1 Samuel 25:2-35

- ■ *Objective:* Children will study 1 Samuel 25:2–35 to discover how Abigail used godly wisdom to prevent a disaster.
- ■ *Materials:* Bible time dress-up box

Choose actors for the parts of David, Nabal, Abigail, and David's men. If you have enough children, two can be donkeys. For the first part of the story, the rest of the class can be sheep and goats. After actors have chosen dress-up items from the box, explain that the children will act out the story as you read it. Encourage them to use facial expressions to portray their characters according to the story. Read slowly and pause as needed for actors to carry out actions.

Nabal was a very rich man in Israel. He had thousands of goats and sheep. Nabal knew a lot about sheep, but he was rude and mean. His wife, Abigail, was clever and beautiful, and she had godly wisdom. David, who was going to become king of Israel, was on the run from King Saul, who wanted to kill David. After running and hiding, David and his loyal friends were hungry and tired. In the custom of Jews, David's men stopped at Nabal's sheep ranch to ask for some food and help.

Do you think Nabal was pleased to give them something to eat? Ha! He was unkind to David's men and even said unfriendly things to them. He refused to give them any food. Nabal had no godly wisdom and didn't know how to make good choices. When the men told David what Nabal had said, David was really mad. He decided to pay back Nabal's unfriendliness by killing him and all his workers!

But when Abigail heard what David was planning and how Nabal had treated him, she jumped right into action. She packed lots of tasty foods onto some donkeys: fresh bread, roasted grain like cereal, some wine, fresh meat, 200 fig cakes, and 100 clusters of raisins. Then Abigail got on a donkey and rode off toward David's camp. Was she going to be in time to stop the killing?

As soon as Abigail saw David, she leaped off her donkey and bowed low to the ground. She gave David much respect and apologized for how Nabal had treated David and his men. "Please forgive me for what happened. Don't take out your anger on those men," she pleaded. "If you do this, God will hold it against you once you become king."

David was amazed at Abigail's words, and he instantly changed his mind about attacking Nabal and his men. He took the wonderful gifts she had brought and told her, "You can go home with a peaceful mind. I'll listen to your advice and do as you ask."

Abigail kept David from killing a bunch of people, and she saved her foolish husband from David's sword too. <u>Abigail's tool for being a winner was using God's wisdom</u>. She made a good choice and saved everyone from a terrible situation.

Use the Clues!
(Bible Review)

We're going to do a review of the Bible story now.

- **What kind of a man was Nabal?** (rude, mean, unfriendly, ungodly)
- **How was Abigail different from her husband?** (she was clever and used godly wisdom to make good choices)
- **How did Abigail show she had godly wisdom?** (she realized what a big problem Nabal caused with David and his men, and thought of a way to solve the problem that worked out for everyone)
- **How do we get God's wisdom?** (ask God for it, read the Bible to learn what God says, memorize Bible verses, learn from the examples of godly people)

Have a child pin ribbon #7 on the winner's jersey. Ask the child to identify the symbol (loaves of bread) and how it's a reminder of this week's Bible story (Abigail used godly wisdom to solve a problem between Nabal and David).

BIBLE MEMORY WAYPOINT   James 1:5
(Scripture Memory)

- **Objective:** *Children will hide God's Word in their hearts for guidance, protection, and encouragement.*
- **Materials:** *cardstock puzzle pieces*

If any of you lacks wisdom, he should ask God, who gives generously to all without finding fault, and it will be given to him (James 1:5).

To help children memorize today's verse, read it aloud from the poster board, then read it with the children as you point to the words. Tell the children the memory verse is hidden around the room as puzzle pieces. Let them find it, allowing each child to discover at least one piece if possible. Then work as a group to assemble the verse. Ask them to read the verse before disassembling the pieces. Divide into two teams and let one team hide puzzle pieces while the other waits outside or hides their eyes. After the second team finds and puts together the puzzle pieces, reverse roles. Each time after the puzzle is assembled, lead the class in reading the verse in unison.

PRAYER STATION

- ■ *Objective: Children will explore and practice prayer for themselves in small groups.*
- ■ *Materials: copies of* StationMaster Card #7 *for each adult or teen helper*

Break into groups of three to five children. Assign a teen or adult helper to each small group and give each helper a copy of *StationMaster Card #7* (see Resources) with ideas for group discussion and prayer.

SNACK STOP: ABIGAIL'S GIFT (Optional)

If you plan to provide a snack, this is an ideal time to serve it.

- ■ *Materials: loaf of bread, raisins, fig-bar cookies*

Ask the children to tell you what food gifts Abigail gave to David and his men. Ask why this was a wise thing to do (because the men had asked Nabal for food and got none). Let them snack on whatever assortment of bread, raisins, and fig cookies you provided, explaining that these snacks are similar to some of the foods people would have eaten in Bible times.

Note: Always be aware of children with food allergies and have another option on hand if necessary.

APPLICATION

- ■ *Objective: Children will have opportunities to show how the lesson works in their own lives through activities and take-home papers.*

Some children's ministries may allow children to play outside at this point. If yours does not, choose one of the following activities.

 **Donkey Race**

- **Materials:** *medium-sized baskets, bungee cords or strips of fabric, 6 or more empty food boxes or containers (such as oatmeal and cereal boxes, cookie tins, plastic peanut butter jars, etc.)*

Divide into two or more teams. You'll need six empty food containers, one basket, and one bungee cord or fabric strip per team. Each team will have to transport their food containers from one location to another by strapping the basket on players who act as the donkeys. Choose starting and ending locations, and add obstacles like chairs that must be circumnavigated. Place half of each team at the start and finish lines, and designate two children from each team to be the donkey and donkey leader. Stack food containers at the starting point. To begin, one player will crouch on all fours while half the team members load the basket with food containers. The donkey leader will take the donkey through the obstacles to the ending point, where the other team members are waiting to unload the donkey. The first team to return to the starting point will be deemed the winners. Play again, allowing new children become the donkey, donkey leader, and loaders/unloaders.

 **Choice Wisdom Chooser**

- **Materials:** *cardstock or heavy-duty paper plates, paper fasteners, large paper clips, markers*

Children will create a spinner-type board that reminds them of places they can find godly wisdom to make the best choices. Have children draw thick marker lines to divide their paper or plate into three equal sections. In each they will draw a picture or write places where they can find wisdom. In one space, they can write or draw a Bible. In another, the name or face of a godly person they know. In the third, create something that reminds them to ask God for wisdom. To make the spinner, they will push a paper fastener through the center of the sheet, with the large paper clip slipped through the fastener prongs. Discuss with children types of situations when they might need godly wisdom. Encourage them to let the spinner remind them to find godly wisdom when they have to make a choice or decision.

 **ON THE FAST TRACK!** *(Take-Home Papers)*

Let children who brought back a signed ticket from last week's take-home paper choose a prize from the treasure box. **Don't forget to ask a parent or guardian to sign your Fast Track! Tickets when you complete the take-home paper. Then you can bring the ticket back and get a prize from the treasure box.**

Distribute the take-home papers and wisdom choosers, if made, just before children leave.

LESSON EIGHT: Popping the Pride Bubble

Memory Verse:
Do nothing out of selfish ambition or vain conceit, but in humility consider others better than yourselves. Each of you should look not only to your own interests, but also to the interests of others **(Philippians 2:3–4)**.

*Early elementary verse in **bold** type.*

Bible Basis:
Luke 18:9–14

Bible Truth:
Winners are humble, not proud.

You Will Need:

- [ ] winner's jersey mounted
- [ ] ribbon #8
- [ ] 1 poster board
- [ ] balloons
- [ ] bubble gum
- [ ] whiteboard
- [ ] permanent marker
- [ ] Bibles
- [ ] shawl or colorful scarf
- [ ] cloth bag with coins inside
- [ ] *On the Fast Track! #8* take-home paper
- [ ] *StationMaster Card #8*
- [ ] *(optional)* treasure box
- [ ] *(optional)* snack: cheese puffs, popcorn, or other "airy" snacks
- [ ] *(optional)* Activity #1: inflated balloons (one per child), contained in large bags if necessary
- [ ] *(optional)* Activity #2: 1" yellow foam balls or yellow pom poms, 2" lengths of black chenille stems, small googly eyes, glue, black elastic thread and craft needle *(optional)*

When you see this icon, it means preparation will take more than five minutes.

GET SET!
(Lesson Preparation)

- ■ Print today's Bible memory verse on a poster board: **Do nothing out of selfish ambition or vain conceit, but in humility consider others better than yourselves. Each of you should look not only to your own interests, but also to the interests of others (Philippians 2:3–4).**
- ■ Photocopy *On the Fast Track! #8* take-home paper for each child.
- ■ Photocopy *StationMaster Card #8* for each helper.
- ■ Blow up four balloons and write a *Use the Clues!* review question on each one with a permanent marker. Blow up additional balloons (one per child) for Activity #1, if using.
- ■ 🌐 Create a Humble Bee sample if using Activity #2.
- ■ Set out the winner's jersey for *Use the Clues!* and *(optional)* treasure box.
- ■ Set up snack and outside play activities if you include these items in your children's ministry.

TICKETS PLEASE!
(Welcome and Bible Connection)

- ■ *Objective: To excite children's interest and connect their own life experiences with the Bible Truth, children will play with balloons and talk about what being humble means.*

Welcome Time Activity: Balloon Volleyball

■ *Materials:* *balloons*

Invite children to bat balloons between themselves and helpers. If enough children are present, play a game of balloon volleyball, using chairs set side by side as a boundary over which players bat the balloon. Helpers can ask children what it means to be humble and if they know anyone they think is humble.

Sharing Time and Bible Connection

■ *Materials:* *four pieces of bubble gum, whiteboard*

When everyone has arrived, call children to the lesson area and welcome them. As you move into the activity and discussion to prepare for the Bible story, give every child the opportunity to say something.

■ **Who can blow a bubble with bubble gum?** Choose four volunteers from those who raise their hands. If not enough children volunteer, ask helpers to step in. Give each volunteer a piece of bubble gum and let them sit down and chew for a few minutes. Meanwhile, engage children in thinking up the opposite of different traits. Write 'afraid' on the board and ask, **What's the opposite of afraid?** Write the most accurate response next to the word. Do the same with 'mad,' 'rude,' and 'greedy.' By this time, the bubble gum should be ready for bubbles. Ask the volunteers to come to the front and blow big bubbles with their gum. Thank them for their efforts.

■ **What made the gum become bubbles?** (air blown into the gum)

■ **What made the bubbles pop?** (too much air)

■ **What might happen if one of our volunteers blew a huge bubble, and then it popped?** (it could stick all over his face, hair, and clothes; it would be a big mess)

　This experiment helps us see a problem we sometimes have. It's called pride, and it's when we get puffed up by how good we think we are, that we're better than others in some way. Write 'pride' on your list of opposites. If you used the Welcome Time Activity, point out that the balloons the children played with are a lot like pride: they are puffed up with a lot of air, but are really just empty inside. **What do you think is the opposite of pride?** If no one knows, leave the space blank for now.

　Today's story shows us about pride and its opposite, and helps us see how God wants winners to be.

ALL ABOARD FOR BIBLE TRUTH

Luke 18:9-14

(Bible Discover and Learn Time)

- **Objective:** *Children will learn from Luke 18:9–14 that the man who prayed for God's help showed humility.*
- **Materials:** *Bibles, scarf or shawl, cloth coin bag*

Hand out the Bibles and ask children to find Luke 18:9. Ask older children to help younger ones. Once everyone has the page, ask six children to each read one verse, starting at verse 9. After reading the text through, children can close their Bibles.

Ask for two boys to model the two men in today's Bible story. Explain that you will mold and form the two as if they were mannequins, or life-sized dolls. Have the boys stand in front of the class, a few feet apart, and be expressionless.

This parable Jesus told shows us the difference between two heart attitudes. One is humility and the other is pride. The two men in the story are examples of these attitudes. Jesus said in his story that two men went to the temple to pray. One was a Pharisee (drape a shawl or scarf over the shoulders of your Pharisee model) **and the other was a tax collector** (put a cloth money bag of coins in his hand). **Pharisees were leaders of the Jewish religion. They were very careful to obey every religious law and custom, and thought they were pretty important. Tax collectors worked for the Romans, who were enemies of the Jews. People didn't like tax collectors because they often cheated people and collected extra money to keep for themselves.**

When the Pharisee came into the temple to pray, he felt like he was such a good Jew and had nothing to confess to God. Move the Pharisee's head to be looking up. **He was proud of keeping all the Jewish customs like giving one tenth of his money to the temple and fasting, or not eating, two times a week.** Lift up the Pharisee's arms and hands like he is praising God. Tell the Pharisee model to give his face an expression of being very proud and better than everyone else.

He prayed, "God, I thank you that I'm not as bad as most of these other people. I'm sure better than that tax collector over there." The Pharisee felt he was better than almost anyone else around him because he did such a great job of keeping every Jewish religious law.

But the tax collector didn't feel that way at all. Move the tax collector's head to look down in humility and submission. **He knew he was sinful and had done wrong. He wouldn't even look up toward heaven because he was aware of how much he needed God's mercy and forgiveness.** Place tax collector's arms over his chest. **This man prayed, "God be merciful to me, a sinner."**

Jesus said that the tax collector was the one who God forgave, because he admitted how sinful he was. The Pharisee felt he was too good to even need forgiveness. But by that very attitude, he sinned against God.

These two men are examples to us of pride (point to Pharisee) **and humility** (point to tax collector). **When God looks at the attitudes in our hearts, He wants to see humility. He wants to see that we know we need Him to forgive us and to help us live the way He wants. A proud heart, like the Pharisee had, is useless to God. <u>No winner in God's kingdom should have an attitude of pride</u>. Winners choose to be humble.**

Write 'humility' opposite 'pride' on the whiteboard list.

Use the Clues!
(Bible Review)

■ **Materials:** *balloons with review questions written on them*

Let's see what you remember.

Bat a balloon with a review question into the group of children. Whoever catches it can read (with help if needed) the question and try to answer. Others can help answer the question too.

Write these questions (in bold) on the balloons:

■ **What did the prideful Pharisee think of himself?** (He felt he was better than others, he kept the laws perfectly, he had nothing sinful to confess)

■ **How was the tax collector humble?** (he was quick to admit his sinfulness, he didn't compare himself to others, he was embarrassed by his wrongdoing and knew he didn't deserve God's mercy)

■ **What kind of attitude does God say a winner will have?** (a humble attitude)

■ **How will we know if we are humble or proud?** (when we're humble, we'll have an attitude of realizing we aren't better than anyone or more special because of our abilities or talents; we will be able to admit our wrongdoing and know we need God's help; if we're proud, we will be too good for others, not admit we do wrong, and refuse to see our mistakes and failures)

Have a child pin ribbon #8 on the winner's jersey. Ask the child to identify the symbol (proud and humble faces) and how it's a reminder of this week's Bible story (the Pharisee was proud, but the tax collector was humble). Review the meanings of the symbols on previous ribbons.

BIBLE MEMORY WAYPOINT
(Scripture Memory)

Philippians 2:3-4

■ **Objective:** *Children will hide God's Word in their hearts for guidance, protection, and encouragement.*

Do nothing out of selfish ambition or vain conceit, but in humility consider others better than yourselves. Each of you should look not only to your own interests, but also to the interests of others (Philippians 2:3–4).

To help children memorize today's verse, read it aloud from the board, then read it with the children as you point to the words. Explain 'selfish ambition' (wanting to do something for your own good instead of for the good of others too) and 'vain conceit' (thinking you're better than others). **To practice being humble, we're going to divide into groups of two to four and help each other learn the verse. We can practice humility by wanting our partners to be successful in memorizing the verse, and not just wanting to learn it ourselves and show how smart we are.** Have children create small mixed-age groups. Circulate to help them work together in memorizing. After several minutes of small group time, have everyone stand and recite the verse together.

PRAYER STATION

- ■ *Objective: Children will explore and practice prayer for themselves in small groups.*
- ■ *Materials: Copies of* StationMaster Card #8 *for each adult or teen helper*

Break into small groups of three to five children. Assign a teen or adult helper to each small group and give each helper a copy of *StationMaster Card #8* (see Resources) with ideas for group discussion and prayer.

SNACK STOP: PUFFED UP SNACKS (Optional)

If you plan to provide a snack, this is an ideal time to serve it.

- ■ *Materials: cheese puffs, popcorn, or other "airy" snacks*

As a reminder that pride puffs us up, you can eat these puffed up snacks. Before you eat, share with a neighbor or friend in class one way it's easy to be proud instead of humble. The next time you eat these kinds of air-puffed foods, remember that Jesus wants our heart attitudes to be humble, not puffed up with pride.
Note: Always be aware of children with food allergies and have another option on hand if necessary.

APPLICATION

■ **Objective:** *Children will have opportunities to show how the lesson works in their own lives through activities and take-home papers.*

Some children's ministries may allow children to play outside at this point. If yours does not, choose one of the following activities.

 ## Balloon Race

■ **Materials:** *inflated balloons (one per child)*

Line up children so two or three can play at a time. They will take a balloon and bat it across the room, then sit on the balloon to pop it. Children with disabilities can work with a partner if possible. Explain that the balloon stands for pride, which we can easily become full of. But pride keeps us from being winners in God's kingdom and ends up making us fall flat, just like the balloon after it's popped.

 ## Humble Beez

■ **Materials:** *1" yellow foam balls or yellow pom poms, 2"lengths of black chenille stems, small googly eyes, glue, black elastic thread and craft needle (optional)*

Create Humble Beez by bending two chenille stems into wing shapes and gluing to the ball on opposite sides. Cut a 2" chenille stem in half and attach two pieces as antennae. Glue on a pair of googly eyes. If desired, thread a needle with black elastic thread and push through bee body from top to bottom. Knot several times under the body and pull back up so knot is snug against bottom of the body. The elastic thread allows the bee to bounce in the air. The bees can be good reminders that winners are humble, not proud.

 ## ON THE FAST TRACK! *(Take-Home Papers)*

Let children who brought back a signed ticket from last week's take-home paper choose a prize from the treasure box. **Don't forget about your *On the Fast Track!* paper for this week. Do the activities and learn your verse. Then have your parent or guardian sign the ticket and bring it back for a prize!**

Distribute the take-home papers and Humble Beez, if made, just before children leave.

LESSON NINE: Follow No Matter What

Memory Verse:

The LORD himself goes before you and will be with you; he **will never leave you** nor forsake you. **Do not be afraid; do not be discouraged** (Deuteronomy 31:8).

*Early elementary verse in **bold** type.*

Bible Basis:

Genesis 37, 39—41

Bible Truth:

Winners follow God no matter what.

You Will Need:

- [ ] winner's jersey
- [ ] ribbon #9
- [ ] 1 poster board
- [ ] butcher paper
- [ ] puppet
- [ ] Bibles
- [ ] whiteboard
- [ ] *On the Fast Track!* #9 take-home paper
- [ ] *StationMaster Card* #9
- [ ] (optional) treasure box
- [ ] (optional) snack: orange slices, raisins, ground cinnamon
- [ ] (optional) Activity #2: card-stock or poster board, scissors, markers, glow-in-the-dark paint or markers (optional)

 *When you see this icon, it means preparation will take more than five minutes.*

 **GET SET!**
(Lesson Preparation)

- ■ Print today's Bible memory verse on a poster board:
  The LORD Himself goes before you and will be with you; he will never leave you nor forsake you. Do not be afraid; do not be discouraged (Deuteronomy 31:8).
- ■ Photocopy *On the Fast Track!* #9 take-home paper for each child.
- ■ Photocopy *StationMaster Card* #9 for each helper.
- ■ Write these verse references on separate slips of paper for use during the Bible story: Genesis 39:2–3, Genesis 39:21–23, Genesis 41:38–40.
- ■ ⏱ Create 12 adult-size footprints. Write the memory verse in segments on the footprints.
- ■ Set out the winner's jersey for *Use the Clues!* and (optional) treasure box.
- ■ Set up snack or outside play activities if you include these items in your children's ministry.

 **TICKETS PLEASE!**
(Welcome and Bible Connection)

- ■ **Objective:** *To excite children's interest and connect their own life experiences with the Bible Truth, children will create a wall mural depicting a difficult journey and talk about their own experiences of hard journeys.*

Welcome Time Activity: Uphill Climb

■ *Materials: butcher paper, markers, puppet*
Put the butcher paper on the floor or mount on the wall at children's height. Introduce them to your puppet and invite them to each create a portion of a journey the puppet will have to travel later in class. Tough spots the puppet might encounter could be quicksand, a landslide, mud, a bees' nest, fork in the road with no direction sign, etc.

Sharing Time and Bible Connection

■ *Materials: puppet*

When everyone has arrived, call children to the lesson area and welcome them. As you move into the activity and discussion to prepare for the Bible story, give every child the opportunity to say something.

If children created a mural in the Welcome Time Activity, use that as the basis of the puppet's difficult time. If no mural was created, think of a series of difficult things the puppet could encounter. Have the puppet dramatically and wearily describe a journey he took, with all its problems and difficulties. Throw in the phrase, "I kept following, no matter what."

■ **What do you think was the worst thing that happened to [puppet] on his journey?**
■ **What is something hard or unexpected that happened to you one time?**
■ **What made [puppet] keep going, no matter what?**

I know of someone named Joseph who, like [puppet], decided to keep going, no matter what. We're going to find out what his reason was and how we can learn to do that, too.

 **ALL ABOARD FOR BIBLE TRUTH**   Genesis 37, 39—41
(Bible Discover and Learn Time)

■ *Objective: Children will explore Genesis 37, 39—41 to learn how Joseph chose to keep following God even when he was mistreated and wrongly imprisoned.*
■ *Materials: Bibles, slips of paper with Bible verse references, whiteboard with large letter "P" written four times vertically*

Hand out Bibles and a verse slip to confident readers and ask them to look up and bookmark the verses. When noted in the story, ask the child with those verses to read it aloud.

Show them the "P" list on the board. **Listen hard to the story, no matter what, and listen for the main things that happened that start with the sound and letter "P". When you hear a main thing that starts with "P," raise your hand. If you're right, we'll add it to our list.** Write each word next to the letter as the words are found.

How many of you have lots of brothers? Today our story is about Joseph, a young man who had ten older brothers. Joseph was also the favorite son of their father, Jacob, and this made the older ten brothers mad. So they decided to get rid of this annoying little brother. When Joseph went out to the sheep meadows to check on his brothers, they jumped on him and threw him in a pit (first "P"). **They didn't know what to do with him, so when they saw some traders on a trip, they sold him as a slave. Joseph was taken away from his home and family to Egypt. But Joseph still chose to follow God.**

In Egypt, Joseph was made a slave to an important man named Potiphar (second "P"). **Potiphar worked for the ruler of Egypt.** Have child with Genesis 39:2–3 read. **Because God was with Joseph, he caused things to go well, and Joseph became a manager for Potiphar.**

Potiphar's wife decided she liked Joseph and wanted to spend time with him, but Joseph knew that was wrong. She was married to another man! He said no, so she got mad and told lies about him to Potiphar. That's how Joseph came to be put in prison (third "P")**—for something he didn't even do!**

Even in prison, Joseph continued to follow God. And God blessed Joseph, so the chief of the prison put him in charge of the other prisoners. Have child with Genesis 39:21–23 read. **God gave Joseph the ability to tell people what their dreams meant. When the ruler of Egypt had scary dreams, someone told him about Joseph, who was still in jail for something he didn't do. The ruler, called Pharaoh, commanded that Joseph come to him to tell him the meaning of his dreams. Joseph could do this because God helped him. Then Pharaoh put Joseph in charge of many things in his kingdom, and he had a lot of power** (fourth "P").

Have child with Genesis 41:38–40 read.

Even when he was mistreated by his brothers and put in prison unfairly, <u>Joseph followed God no matter what</u>. That makes him a winner, and a great example for us.

Use the Clues!
(Bible Review)

Let's review the story!

■ **What were unfair or hard things that happened to Joseph?** (his brothers threw him in a pit and then sold him to slave traders, he was put in jail unfairly, Potiphar's wife accused him of something he didn't do)

■ **Why did God continue to help Joseph in these hard times?** (Joseph chose to keep following God, no matter what happened)

■ **How did God bless and help Joseph?** (He saved him from death, put him in an important man's house, gave him good jobs, gave him the ability to tell what dreams meant, caused him to become an important person in Egypt)

■ **How can we follow Joseph's example?** (choose to keep following God no matter what things come along)

■ **What sorts of things could make us want to go a different direction than God wants?** (losing friends, family problems, bad sickness, death of a person we love, being made fun of for being a Christian, etc.)

Have a child pin ribbon #9 on the winner's jersey. Ask the child to identify the symbol (jail cell) and how it's a reminder of this week's Bible story (Joseph kept following God despite being mistreated and unfairly punished). Review the symbols from previous weeks with the children.

BIBLE MEMORY WAYPOINT
(Scripture Memory)

Deuteronomy 31:8

■ **Objective:** *Children will hide God's Word in their hearts for guidance, protection, and encouragement.*

■ **Materials:** *footprints with verse portions*

The LORD himself goes before you and will be with you; he will never leave you nor forsake you. Do not be afraid; do not be discouraged (Deuteronomy 31:8).

To help children memorize today's verse, read it aloud from the board, then read it with the children as you point to the words. Hand out the footprints with verse words and have the children put them in order according to the verse poster. Then ask them to work as a team to make a pathway around the room, taping footprints to the floor in correct verse order. When the verse pathway is complete, ask one child to lead and the others to follow. The leader will say the verse in phrases as he/she walks along the path (and even make up actions if he/she so chooses), and those who are following will echo it. Repeat a couple of times with new leaders.

PRAYER STATION

■ **Objective:** *Children will explore and practice prayer for themselves in small groups.*
■ **Materials:** *copies of* StationMaster Card #9 *for each adult or teen helper*

Break into small groups of three to five children. Assign a teen or adult helper to each small group and give each helper a copy of *StationMaster Card #9* (see Resources) with ideas for group discussion and prayer.

SNACK STOP: EGYPTIAN TREAT (Optional)

If you plan to provide a snack, this is an ideal time to serve it.

■ **Materials:** *orange slices, raisins, ground cinnamon*

Ask children what country Joseph was taken to as a slave. In Egypt, spiced oranges and raisins are a treat. Hand out some of both fruits to the children. Ask each if he/she wants a sprinkle of cinnamon on the orange slices.

Note: Always be aware of children with food allergies and have another option on hand if necessary.

APPLICATION

■ **Objective:** *Children will have opportunities to show how the lesson works in their own lives through activities and take-home papers.*

Some children's ministries may allow children to play outside at this point. If yours does not, choose one of the following activities.

 ## Train Game

Before you begin, designate a start and finish line. **Trains often pull really heavy loads. Sometimes it looks like they won't make it, but the engines keep tugging no matter what! Today, we're going to play a train game.** Divide children into equal teams and have them file behind the starting line. The first player in each team runs across the finish line and back; the second player "hooks on" and both run across the line and back. This continues until all of the players are in line aboard the "train." The first team to cross the starting line wins.

 ## Footprint Poster

■ *Materials: cardstock or poster board, scissors, markers, glow-in-the-dark paint or markers (optional)*

Have children take turns standing on a piece of cardstock while another student traces both feet (with or without shoes). When everyone's feet have been traced, children will cut out their outlined shapes and write on them "I'll follow God even when…" and complete the sentence with a statement of something that is hard or uncertain (for example: "I move to a new town" or "my dad is looking for a job"). Encourage children one-on-one to think of times they would be tempted to not follow God because the situation is discouraging or scary. Share places they can display their footprint posters as reminders to be winners by following God no matter what.

 ## ON THE FAST TRACK! *(Take-Home Papers)*

Let children who brought back a signed ticket from last week's take-home paper choose a prize from the treasure box. **Here are your *On the Fast Track!* papers for this week. Don't forget to have your parent or guardian sign your ticket after you've done the activities and memorized the verse. Then next week, you can choose a prize from the treasure box!**

Distribute the take-home papers and paper feet (if made) just before children leave.

LESSON TEN: A Heart of Caring

Memory Verse:
Serve wholeheartedly, as if you were serving the Lord, not men (Ephesians 6:7).

Bible Basis:
Luke 19:1–10

Bible Truth:
Winners care for those around them.

Care for Others!

You Will Need:

- [ ] winner's jersey
- [ ] ribbon #10
- [ ] Bibles
- [ ] Bible time dress-up box
- [ ] sturdy chair
- [ ] whiteboard
- [ ] ball
- [ ] CD/tape player and music CD/tape
- [ ] *On the Fast Track! #10* take-home paper
- [ ] *StationMaster Card #10*
- [ ] (optional) treasure box
- [ ] (optional) snack: fish crackers, yogurt, spoons, baby carrots, paper plates, napkins, paper cups, water
- [ ] (optional) Activity #1: homemade signs, tape
- [ ] (Optional) Activity #2: paper, markers or crayons, pencils, envelopes, stickers (optional)

 **When you see this icon, it means preparation will take more than five minutes.**

 **GET SET!**
(Lesson Preparation)

- Print today's Bible memory verse on a whiteboard: **Serve wholeheartedly, as if you were serving the Lord, not men (Ephesians 6:7).**
- Photocopy *On the Fast Track! #10* take-home paper for each child.
- Photocopy *StationMaster Card #10* for each helper.
- Make four photocopies of the Bible story script.
- If using the Welcome Time Activity, write slips of paper with ideas about people who care for others. Ideas: teachers, nurses, doctors, police officers, fire fighters, pastors, parents, grandparents, coaches.
- Set out the winner's jersey for *Use the Clues!* and *(optional)* treasure box.
- Set up snack and outside play activities if you include these items in your children's ministry.
- Write the following words on pieces of 8½" x 11" paper to be sign pairs if using Activity #1: thirsty, drink, hungry, food, sick, doctor, cold, clothes, etc.

 **TICKETS PLEASE!**
(Welcome and Bible Connection)

- *Objective: To excite children's interest and connect their own life experiences with the Bible Truth, children will play a drawing game to start thinking about caring for others.*

Welcome Time Activity: Who Cares?

■ *Materials: slips of paper with drawing ideas*
As children arrive, invite them to the white or chalk board where the group will play a drawing game. Using their own ideas or a stock of prepared ones, they will draw pictures of people who care for others. As they draw, the rest of the group will try to guess the type of person they're drawing.

Sharing Time and Bible Connection

When everyone has arrived, call children to the lesson area and welcome them. As you move into the activity and discussion to prepare for the Bible story, give every child the opportunity to say something.

Start the discussion by taking an informal poll.

■ **If you've ever sent someone a card to show you care about them, stand up.** Thank children, and have them sit again.
■ **If you've made a gift for someone you love, raise your hand.** Thank children again.
■ **If you've gone to see someone who is sick or needy, clap your hands three times.** Thank those who clapped.
■ **If you've smiled at someone who was having a bad day or who was sad, stand up and stomp your feet two times.** Thank children.

I can see that all of you have shown care in the past. Caring for those around us isn't just a nice thing to do, it's what God asks us to do. It's what winners in God's kingdom choose to do. We're going to read about someone who shows us more about caring for others.

 # ALL ABOARD FOR BIBLE TRUTH

Luke 19:1–10

(Bible Discover and Learn Time)

■ **Objective:** *Children will hear the story in Luke 19:1–10 to find out how Jesus showed Zacchaeus that he cared about him.*
■ **Materials:** *Bibles, Bible time dress-up box, chair, 4 photocopies of the Bible story script*

Choose two or more students to be the "crowd," one student to be Zacchaeus, and one student to be Jesus. Have the actors put on clothes from the Bible time dress-up box and have a sturdy chair handy to be a "tree." Hand actors copies of the script and ask them to act out the story as scripted.

Crowd Member 1: **Wow! The streets of Jericho sure are busy today. I guess everyone wants to see Jesus.**

Crowd Member 2: **Yeah. I sure do!** (*meanly*) **Oh, look. There's Zacchaeus. I thought he'd be at home counting his money. Or should I say, *our money*.**

Crowd Member 1: **I'm surprised that tax collector shows his face in public. No one likes him.**

Zacchaeus: (*jumps up and down like he's trying to see over people's heads*) **I can't see over all of these people.**

Crowd Member 2: **Ha! He's so short, he can't see over the crowd.**

Crowd Member 1: **Look—Jesus is coming!**

(*Jesus starts walking down the "road."*)

(*Zacchaeus runs and jumps up on the chair behind the two crowd members.*)

(*Crowd Members cheer as Jesus comes closer to them.*)

(*Jesus stops in front of the crowd members.*)

Crowd Member 2: (*excited*) **I think Jesus is going to talk to us! We are so special.**

Crowd Member 1: **This is the best day of my life. I hope he likes my new robe.**

Jesus: **Zacchaeus.**

Zacchaeus: **Jesus knows my name?**

Jesus: **Come down from that tree. I want to come to your house today.**

Crowd Member 2: **Did Jesus just say what I thought he said? Doesn't he know that Zacchaeus is a cheater?**

Crowd Member 1: **I can't believe it. Jesus just looked right over us to that tax collector, that—that *sinner*, and said he wanted to go to *his* house?**

Zacchaeus: **Jesus wants to come to *my* house? He actually cares about me? Praise the Lord! Someone cares! *Jesus* cares! He wants to come to my house!** (*Jumps down from the chair and runs to kneel in front of Jesus*) **Lord! Here and now I give half of everything I own to the poor, and if I** have cheated anybody out of anything, I will pay back four times the amount!

Jesus: **Today, you are saved, my friend, because** (*turns toward the crowd members*) **this man too is one of God's people. I have not come to spend time with people who think they have it all together. I have come to find and care for those who are hurting and lost and unloved.**

Use the Clues!
(Bible Review)

- **Materials:** *ball, CD/tape player and music CD/tape*

Let's do some fun review of the story!

Play a game for the review time. With children in a circle, turn on some music and have children roll or kick a ball around. Turn off the music randomly. Whoever kicked or touched the ball last answers the question.

- **Why did the crowd members dislike Zacchaeus so much?** (he was a tax collector who, most likely, had cheated them out of money)
- **What did Jesus say that shocked the crowd members?** (He called to Zacchaeus and told him He wanted to go to his house)
- **Why did Jesus want to go to Zacchaeus' house?** (Jesus cared about Zacchaeus; he came to be with people who are hurting, lost, and have sinned)
- **Do you know any hurting, lost, or unloved people?** (prompt children to think about lonely classmates or neighbors, elderly people who have lost their families, homeless people, etc.)

Have a child pin ribbon #10 on the winner's jersey. Ask the child to identify the symbol (man in a tree) and how it's a reminder of this week's Bible story (Jesus wants us to show others we care about them). Ask volunteers to help you review the symbols from previous weeks.

BIBLE MEMORY WAYPOINT
(Scripture Memory)

Ephesians 6:7

- **Objective:** *Children will hide God's Word in their hearts for guidance, protection, and encouragement.*
- **Materials:** *whiteboard*

Serve wholeheartedly, as if you were serving the Lord, not men (Ephesians 6:7).

To help children memorize today's verse, read it aloud from the board, then read it with the children as you point to the words. Choose a student to come and erase one wordd, and have the class read the verse again. Then choose a different student to come and erase another word. Continue until all of the words are erased and children can say the verse without any visual help.

PRAYER STATION

- ■ *Objective:* *Children will explore and practice prayer for themselves in small groups.*
- ■ *Materials:* *Copies of* StationMaster Card #10 *for each adult or teen helper*

Break into small groups of three to five children. Assign a teen or adult helper to each small group and give each helper a copy of *StationMaster Card #10* (see Resources) with ideas for group discussion and prayer.

SNACK STOP: ZACCHAEUS' DINNER PARTY (Optional)

If you plan to provide a snack, this is an ideal time to serve it.

- ■ *Materials:* *fish crackers, yogurt, spoons, baby carrots, paper plates, napkins, paper cups, water*

Have some children prepare a "dinner" for the class by setting the table with paper plates, spoons, napkins, and cups of water. Then have different volunters serve the fish crackers, yogurt, and carrots. Others can help clean up. Talk about how important it is to show other people that we care for them.

Note: Always be aware of children with food allergies and have another option on hand if necessary.

APPLICATION

- ■ *Objective:* *Children will have opportunities to show how the lesson works in their own lives through activities and take-home papers.*

Some children's ministries may allow children to play outside at this point. If yours does not, choose one of the following activities.

 **Caring Search**

■ **Materials:** *signs, tape*

Tape a sign on each child's back and have everyone go around the room and ask yes or no questions to figure out what their sign says. Once they know who they are, they need to find their match (i.e., hungry goes with food, thirsty goes with drink, etc.) When they are paired up, each pair should sit down together and tell each other something that each really likes about the other person.

 **Caring Coupons**

■ **Materials:** *paper, markers or crayons, pencils, envelopes, stickers (optional)*

Challenge students to make coupons to give to family members and others they know, offering to do a caring act for them. Let children choose the ways they want to show they care, such as doing a chore for a sibling, giving time to help someone, giving a backrub, etc. Ask children to create at least two coupons, though more are even better. Put each child's coupons in an envelope to take home.

 **ON THE FAST TRACK!** *(Take-Home Papers)*

Let children who brought back a signed ticket from last week's take-home paper choose a prize from the treasure box. **Here's your *On the Fast Track!* paper for this week. When you complete the activities and memorize the verse, have a parent or guardian sign the ticket. Bring it back next week to choose a prize from the treasure box!**

If the children made caring coupons, distribute them along with the take-home papers before children leave.

LESSON ELEVEN: To Tell the Truth

Memory Verse:

Love does not delight in evil but rejoices with the truth (1 Corinthians 13:6).

Bible Basis:

Genesis 27 and 33

Bible Truth:

Winners choose to be truthful.

Be Truthful!

You Will Need:

- [ ] winner's jersey
- [ ] ribbon #11
- [ ] 1 poster board
- [ ] large sheet of white and of black paper
- [ ] white crayon or marker
- [ ] whiteboard
- [ ] 4 pieces of furry material
- [ ] bowl
- [ ] plain shirt
- [ ] On the Fast Track! #11 take-home paper
- [ ] StationMaster Card #11
- [ ] (optional) treasure box
- [ ] (optional) snack: pretzels, raisins or dried cranberries, mini crackers, cereal O's, mini marshmallows, paper cups or bowls
- [ ] (optional) Activity #1: heavy-duty or nylon thread, weighty objects like metal washers, tape, index cards, markers or pencils
- [ ] (optional) Activity #2: ball of yarn or string

When you see this icon, it means preparation will take more than five minutes.

GET SET!
(Lesson Preparation)

- ■ Print today's Bible memory verse on a poster board: **Love does not delight in evil but rejoices with the truth (1 Corinthians 13:6).**
- ■ Photocopy *On the Fast Track! #11* for each child.
- ■ Photocopy *StationMaster Card #11* for each helper.
- ■ Write TRUTH in block letters on a large white sheet of paper, and LIE in white block letters on a large black sheet. Mount on two different walls for the Welcome Time Activity.
- ■ Set out the winner's jersey for *Use the Clues!* and (optional) treasure box.
- ■ Set up snack and outside play activities if you include these items in your children's ministry.

TICKETS PLEASE!
(Welcome and Bible Connection)

- ■ **Objective:** *To excite children's interest and connect their own life experiences with the Bible Truth, children will play a game that challenges them to discern between truth and lies.*

Welcome Time Activity: Truth or Lie

■ *Materials: white paper labeled TRUTH, black paper labeled LIE*
To play this game, have everyone start at the TRUTH wall. Children will run to the side that stands for whatever you tell them. If you say "It's rainy outside" and it is, they should race to stand along the white TRUTH wall. If you state "Dogs wear rain hats," they race to the black LIE wall. Use both fun and serious statements, including some basic ones about God and the Bible.

Sharing Time and Bible Connection
■ *Materials: whiteboard*

When everyone has arrived, call children to the lesson area and welcome them. As you move into the activity and discussion to prepare for the Bible story, give every child the opportunity to say something.

■ **Who can tell me the difference between a truth and a lie?**
Truth is something that is fully honest. A lie is something that is even a little bit not true. Let's say a lie is a dark mark on this whiteboard.
Ask a volunteer to tell you something that is a HUGE lie. Ask the child to then draw a thick, long line on the whiteboard to stand for the lie. Ask another child to tell you something that's a lie, but not as big. Let that child erase part of the line. Continue doing this until you have a small section of the line left.

■ **What's a white lie?** Let children respond.
Many people think a white lie is just a tiny bit of untruth, but that it's not wrong as long as it doesn't hurt anyone. This line up here is a white lie, like telling your dad that you've brushed your teeth when you're really just *planning* to brush your teeth but haven't gotten to it yet. It seems like your words aren't really bad, but are they true? No! The mark is still on the board because a white lie is a lie just like any other untrue words. God wants winners in his kingdom to learn to be completely truthful, not just mostly truthful. Let's see how some people in the Bible show us what God means.

ALL ABOARD FOR BIBLE TRUTH

(Bible Discover and Learn Time)

Genesis 27 and 33

■ *Objective: Children will learn from Genesis 27 and 33 how lies tore a family apart.*
■ *Materials: 4 pieces of furry material, bowl, plain shirt*

As we find out how lies destroyed a family in today's Bible story, your job is to listen for the lies. When you hear someone in the Bible story saying or doing anything untruthful, raise your hand.

Choose children to be Isaac, Jacob, Esau, and Rebekah. Give the furry fabric to Rebekah. **You act out the story as I tell it.**

Isaac was an old man. He told his oldest son, Esau, "Get your bow and arrows and go hunting. Make a good stew for me from the meat you bring back. After I eat it, I want to bless you before I die." Blessings were very important in Bible times. The oldest son got the blessing and it was more valuable than money.

Rebekah, Isaac's wife, heard Isaac. Rebekah wanted the younger son, Jacob, to get the blessing. So she made up a plan to cheat Esau. If children didn't catch it, prompt them that cheating is being untruthful.

Rebekah called Jacob. "Go get two young goats. I'll make your father's favorite food. Then you can take it to him and get the blessing."

Jacob knew the blessing belonged to Esau. He should have said no. Instead he said. "But Esau has a lot of hair on his body, and I don't. If father touches me, he'll know it's me and not Esau. He might curse me instead of blessing me."

"Trust me," said Rebekah.

So Jacob got the meat and Rebekah made Isaac's favorite food.

Then Rebekah covered Jacob's hands and neck with goatskins. Place furry fabric on Jacob's arms. **She told him to wear Esau's best clothes** (put on shirt). **Then she gave him the food** (use the bowl), **and he went to Isaac's tent. Jacob pretended to be Esau so he could trick his father.**

"Who is it?" asked Isaac.

"It's me, Esau," said Jacob.

"How did you find the wild game so quickly?" asked Isaac.

"The Lord your God gave it to me," said Jacob. Did Jacob have wild meat? No, he had goat meat from their herd.

Isaac was so old he couldn't see well. "Come here so I can make sure you're Esau," said Isaac. "You sound like Jacob." Isaac felt the goatskin that Rebekah had tied to Jacob. "But you feel like Esau. Are you really Esau?"

"Yes," Jacob lied again.

After Isaac ate, he blessed Jacob. Then Jacob hurried away. Right then Esau came back with stew made from the meat he hunted (use bowl again). When he found that his brother had lied and stolen his blessing, Esau hated Jacob. He cried hard because he had lost the precious blessing he should have had.

Esau said to himself, "After my father dies and we have mourned, I'm going to kill my brother."

When Rebekah heard him say this, she told Jacob to pack his clothes and run away. Because Rebekah and Jacob both lied and did untruthful things, Isaac felt betrayed, Esau hated Jacob, Jacob had to leave home, and he would never see his mother again. Their family was hurt for a long time.

How many ways did you count Jacob and Rebekah lying and being untruthful? (five) Go through the story to point out the lies and dishonesty. Rebekah's plan to cheat Esau, Jacob agreeing to cheat Esau, Jacob saying he was Esau two times, Jacob saying he had hunted wild meat that was actually goat meat.

God hates lies and untruthful actions. <u>Winners always tell and live the truth</u>. Even if someone else suggests the lie or wrong action, if we do it, like Jacob did, we're guilty ourselves.

Use the Clues!
(Bible Review)

It's time for a little review of the Bible story.

- **What did Isaac want to give Esau?** (a blessing)
- **How did Jacob get the blessing instead?** (he followed Rebekah's plan to cheat Esau by pretending to be him)
- **Who else was untruthful besides Jacob?** (Rebekah, for suggesting the plan and helping Jacob cheat Isaac)
- **What problems happened because Jacob and Rebekah were untruthful?** (Esau hated his brother, Esau was cheated of his blessing, Isaac was hurt, Jacob had to run away to keep from being killed by Esau)
- **What does God say we need to do to be winners in His kingdom?** (only say and live ways that are truthful, never untruthful)

Have a child pin ribbon #11 on the winner's jersey. Ask the child to identify the symbol (hairy arms) and how it's a reminder of this week's Bible story (Jacob and Rebekah were untruthful and hurt their family). Ask a volunteer to help you review all the symbols from previous weeks.

BIBLE MEMORY WAYPOINT
(Scripture Memory)   1 Corinthians 13:6

- *Objective: Children will hide God's Word in their hearts for guidance, protection, and encouragement.*

Love does not delight in evil but rejoices with the truth (1 Corinthians 13:6).

To help children memorize today's verse, read it aloud from the poster, then read it with the children as you point to the words. Practice the verse by clapping with the words as you say the words, leading the children to clap and repeat the words back. Then break into different groups, such as girls and boys, older kids and younger kids, those wearing green and everyone else. One group claps and says the first half, with the second group clapping and saying the remainder of the verse. Ask children for other ideas on how to divide the group for the two-part rehearsal.

 ## PRAYER STATION

■ *Objective:* *Children will explore and practice prayer for themselves in small groups.*
■ *Materials:* *copies of* StationMaster Card #11 *for each adult or teen helper*

Break into groups of three to five children. Assign a teen or adult helper to each small group and give each helper a copy of *StationMaster Card #11* (see Resources) with ideas for group discussion and prayer.

 ## SNACK STOP: SAVORY STEW (Optional)

If you plan to provide a snack, this is an ideal time to serve it.

■ *Materials:* *pretzels, raisins or dried cranberries, mini crackers, cereal O's, mini marshmallows, paper cups or bowls*

Let children concoct their own savory "stew" by mixing in a bowl or cup various amounts of the snack foods you provide.

Note: Always be aware of children with food allergies and have another option on hand if necessary.

 ## APPLICATION

■ *Objective:* *Children will have opportunities to show how the lesson works in their own lives through activities and take-home papers.*

Some children's ministries may allow children to play outside at this point. If yours does not, choose one of the following activities.

Plumb Line

■ **Materials:** *heavy-duty or nylon thread, weighty objects like metal washers, tape, index cards, markers or pencils*

Explain and demonstrate the usefulness of a plumb line. It shows if something is straight and true, like a window or doorframe. Builders use plumb lines to make sure what they build is straight, so it's more solid and even. Children will make a plumb line to remind them that winners choose to be truthful. Tie a metal washer to one end of a 12" length of thread. Write the Bible Truth, *winners choose to be truthful,* on the index card. Tape the free end of the thread to the back of the card. Challenge children to think about their words and actions this week, using the plumb line as a reminder to be truthful.

Web of Lies

■ **Materials:** *ball of yarn or string*

Explain that this activity shows us how we can get caught in even the smallest lies, and that speaking or acting untruthfully has consequences. Have the children stand in a loose cluster. Large classes can do this activity in two or more groups. Hand the ball of yarn to one child who will give an example of a lie or untruthful act. Then the child tosses the yarn to a child across the group, who adds another example. As children toss the yarn around, the group will be tangled in a web. After each child has given at least one example of a lie or untruthful action, ask for their observations on the situation. Lying and acting untruthfully create consequences and trap you and others in sin.

ON THE FAST TRACK! *(Take-Home Papers)*

Let children who brought back a signed ticket from last week's take-home paper choose a prize from the treasure box. **Here are your *On the Fast Track!* papers for this week. When you finish your activities and learn your verse, have your parent or guardian sign the ticket. Then bring it back next week for a prize from the treasure box!**

Distribute the take-home papers and plumb lines, if made, just before children leave.

LESSON TWELVE: How Can I Help?

Faith In Action!

Memory Verse:

I will show you my faith by what I do (James 2:18).

Bible Basis:

Joshua 2 and 6:22–25

Bible Truth:

Winners put their faith into action.

You Will Need:

- [ ] winner's jersey
- [ ] ribbon #12
- [ ] 1 poster board
- [ ] ping pong balls or other light-weight balls
- [ ] inflated beach ball or other large, lightweight ball
- [ ] string
- [ ] rubber bands
- [ ] Bible
- [ ] Rahab and 2 spies puppets
- [ ] yellow yarn
- [ ] red cord
- [ ] puppet stage (sheet draped over two chairs)
- [ ] *On the Fast Track! #12* take-home paper
- [ ] *StationMaster Card #12*
- [ ] *(optional)* treasure box
- [ ] *(optional)* snack: red licorice, crackers
- [ ] *(optional)* Activity #1: balls, bean-bags or wads of paper, whiteboard or poster board
- [ ] *(optional)* Activity #2: copies of puppets, scissors, glue, craft sticks, markers and/or colored pencils

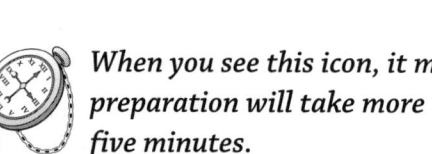

When you see this icon, it means preparation will take more than five minutes.

GET SET!
(Lesson Preparation)

- ◼ Print today's Bible memory verse on a poster board: **I will show you my faith by what I do (James 2:18).**
- ◼ Photocopy *On the Fast Track! #12* take-home paper for each child.
- ◼ Photocopy *StationMaster Card #12* for each helper.
- ◼  Enlarge Rahab and 2 spies images (see Resources), cut out, color, and mount them on rulers for use in the for Bible story section.
- ◼ Draw 6" red circles or Xs on the whiteboard or poster board if using Activity #1.
- ◼ Photocopy Rahab and spies puppets (see Resources) for each child if using Activity #2.
- ◼ Set out the winner's jersey for *Use the Clues!* and *(optional)* treasure box.
- ◼ Set up snack and outside play activities if you include these items in your children's ministry.

TICKETS PLEASE!
(Welcome and Bible Connection)

- ◼ *Objective:* To excite children's interest and connect their own life experiences with the Bible Truth, children will experiment with ways to move a ball and share what they think it means to "put feet to their faith."

Welcome Time Activity: Ball Track

■ **Materials:** *ping pong balls or other lightweight balls, string, rubber bands*
Mark an X at one end of a table. Set the balls on the table and the other materials nearby. Tell children that for this game, they need to make the ball move over the X without touching the ball with their hands. Let them use creative ideas to accomplish this task. Discuss what it means to "put feet to your faith" and provide a few examples for children to ponder.

Sharing Time and Bible Connection

■ **Materials:** *inflated beach ball or similar large, lightweight ball*

When everyone has arrived, call children to the lesson area and welcome them. As you move into the activity and discussion to prepare for the Bible story, give every child the opportunity to say something.

Toss the beach ball into the group of kids and tell them they should tap it up and around the group as you brainstorm types of sports where the player has to use his or her feet. Once they've run out of ideas, retrieve the ball.

It seems like for many sports, a player needs to use his or her feet. I can't think how a soccer player could do very well without moving around the field by running, or how hard it would be for a swimmer to swim without being able to kick his feet for more speed. Just like a player needs to make his feet work to win at his sport, we need to put our faith to work to do our best for God's kingdom. We could say that being winners for God means putting feet to our faith. In the story we're about to hear together, we'll see how one lady put faith to her feet.

 # ALL ABOARD FOR BIBLE TRUTH   Joshua 2, 6:22–25
(Bible Discover and Learn Time)

■ **Objective:** *Children will discover from Joshua 2 and 6:22–25 how Rahab helped the Israelite spies and was later saved from destruction.*
■ **Materials:** *Bible, Rahab and 2 spies puppets, yellow yarn, red cord, puppet stage (sheet draped over 2 chairs)*

Choose three children to be puppeteers and act out the story as you tell it. You will need a Rahab and two spies. Choose one confident reader and have him or her mark Joshua 2:12–13 and Joshua 6:23–25.

How many of you live near a wall? Do any of you have a house in a wall? In the book of Joshua, a woman named Rahab had a house inside a wall of the city of Jericho. Enter Rahab. Big cities in Bible times had very thick, sturdy walls to protect the people from their enemies. Jericho's wall was so thick, people like Rahab could live in the wall itself.

This woman Rahab wasn't an Israelite, but she had heard about how the God of the Israelites had done amazing things. She believed He was the true God. And she put feet to her faith by acting on what she believed.

Joshua was the Israelite leader after Moses. God told Joshua to take over the city of Jericho. So Joshua sent two spies into the city to find out what their protection and soldiers were like. Enter spies. But the king of Jericho found out about the spies. He sent out soldiers to find them. The spies needed to hide. They knocked on a door. Knock on a table or wall. A woman named Rahab answered the door. She let them hide in her house. Rahab decided to have them hide on her roof under bundles of flax. Have the Rahab puppet put the yellow yarn over the two spies.

The next morning, she made a deal with the two Israelite spies. Have your reader read Joshua 2:12–13. The spies agreed. "If you don't tell that we were here, we'll make sure you're saved when God destroys this city," they told Rahab.

Rahab helped the men escape from Jericho by letting them climb down the wall using a rope. She said they would know where she lived because of the red cord tied in her window. Have Rahab let down the red cord for the spies. Exit spies.

Not long after, God told Joshua how to conquer Jericho. God broke down the thick, heavy walls of the city. He told them to destroy everyone in the city, except Rahab and her family. They knew where she lived because they could see the red cord in the window. Have your reader read Joshua 6:23–25.

Because <u>Rahab put her faith into action</u>, she was saved. Like any winner in God's kingdom, showing our faith in action is the only way to win. Exit Rahab.

Use the Clues!
(Bible Review)

I'm going to ask some questions about today's story.
Raise your hand if you know the answer.

- **Why did the spies go into Jericho?** (to find out about the city so they could attack it)
- **Why did Rahab help the spies?** (she had heard of the miracles God had done for the Israelites and she believed in their God)
- **What promise did the spies make to Rahab?** (that if she didn't tell the king's men about them, they would be sure she was be saved when the city was destroyed)
- **Why was Rahab and her family saved from Jericho but everyone else in the city died?** (Rahab had faith in God and acted on her faith to save the Israelite spies)

- **How was Rahab a winner?** (she used her faith to work for God's kingdom)
- **What kinds of things can we do to show our faith in action?** (help people because we know God loves them, say things that are encouraging and honest because we know that pleases God)

Have a child pin ribbon #12 on the winner's jersey. Ask the child to identify the symbol (red cord) and how it's a reminder of this week's Bible story (Rahab had faith in God and helped His spies and was saved when Jericho was destroyed). **Would anyone like to tell me what these other ribbons stand for?** Give a few volunteers the opportunity to help you review the symbols from previous weeks.

BIBLE MEMORY WAYPOINT
(Scripture Memory)

James 2:18

- ***Objective:*** *Children will hide God's Word in their hearts for guidance, protection, and encouragement.*

I will show you my faith by what I do (James 2:18).

To help children memorize today's verse, read it aloud from the board, then read it with the children as you point to the words. Have children make small groups and create a cheer or chant with the verse. After several minutes, ask each group to demonstrate their cheer or chant.

PRAYER STATION

- **Objective:** *Children will explore and practice prayer for themselves in small groups.*
- **Materials:** *copies of* StationMaster Card #12 *for each adult or teen helper*

Break into small groups of three to five children. Assign a teen or adult helper to each small group and give each helper a copy of *StationMaster Card #12* (see Resources) with ideas for group discussion and prayer.

SNACK STOP: RED CORDS (Optional)

If you plan to provide a snack, this is an ideal time to serve it.

- **Materials:** *red licorice, crackers*

Have children build their own wall with a handful of crackers and display their red licorice on the wall like the red cord Rahab used. Talk about what Rahab might have wondered or worried about after she helped the spies escape. **How does our faith help us when we're worried?**

Note: Always be aware of children with food allergies and have another option on hand if necessary.

APPLICATION

- **Objective:** *Children will have opportunities to show how the lesson works in their own lives through activities and take-home papers.*

Some children's ministries may allow children to play outside at this point. If yours does not, choose one of the following activities.

 **Jericho Wall Target Practice**

- **Materials:** *balls, beanbags or wads of paper, red circles or Xs drawn on a whiteboard or poster board*

Children will toss balls at the "wall" and try to hit a circle or X. This game can be played with teams or with the class as a whole. Make a tape line behind which children stand to toss their balls. Give each child three tosses per turn. Two or three players can toss at a time. Remind children that in the battle of Jericho, God knocked the wall down, not people.

 **Stick Puppets**

- **Materials:** *copies of puppets (see Resources), scissors, glue, craft sticks, markers and/or colored pencils*

Children will make their own set of Rahab and spies puppets to remind them to put their faith into action. Allow children to color the puppets. Then cut them out and mount them on craft sticks. As you work, encourage children to talk about ways they have put their faith into action in the past and how they plan to do so in the future.

 **ON THE FAST TRACK!** *(Take-Home Papers)*

If you brought a signed ticket today, come up and choose something from the treasure box! Don't forget to do the activities this week. Remind children to have their parents or guardian sign the ticket when they finish the activities.

Distribute the take-home papers and puppets, if made, just before children leave.

LESSON THIRTEEN: Winning the Prize

Memory Verse:

Those who hope in the LORD will renew their strength. They will soar on wings like eagles; they will run and not grow weary, they will walk and not be faint **(Isaiah 40:31).**

*Early elementary verse in **bold** type.*

Bible Basis:

Luke 12:16–21

Bible Truth:

Winners know that the real prize is being rich in character.

You Will Need:

- [ ] winner's jersey
- [ ] ribbon #13
- [ ] 1 poster board
- [ ] small golf-sized balls
- [ ] cardboard wrapping paper tubes or toy hockey sticks/golf clubs
- [ ] paper cups
- [ ] masking tape
- [ ] Bibles
- [ ] building blocks
- [ ] ribbon *(optional)*
- [ ] *On the Fast Track! #13* take-home paper
- [ ] *StationMaster Card #13*
- [ ] *(optional)* treasure box
- [ ] *(optional)* snack: orange juice or sports drinks, fruit slices, cheese sticks or chunks, granola bars
- [ ] *(optional)* Activity #1: medium- to large-size sturdy paper cups, 3" hard foam balls, craft or tempera paint in primary colors (red and/or blue are best), brushes, cardboard cut in 6" x 8" rectangles, gold and silver star stickers, glue and glue sticks, scissors, pins, colored construction paper
- [ ] *(optional)* Activity #2: toy bowling set or 10 empty 2-liter bottles and a ball (one set per group)

GET SET!

(Lesson Preparation)

- Print today's Bible memory verse on a poster board:

  Those who hope in the LORD will renew their strength. They will soar on wings like eagles; they will run and not grow weary, they will walk and not be faint (Isaiah 40:31).

- Photocopy *On the Fast Track #13* take-home paper for each child.
- Photocopy *StationMaster Card #13* for each helper.
- Make a masking tape starting line and tape a paper cup 4'–5' away for the Welcome Time Activity.
- If you'd like, create a winner's ribbon as an end-of-book award for each child using the template in the Resources section and 14" long pieces of ribbon.
- Set out the winner's jersey for *Use the Clues!* and *(optional)* treasure box.
- Set up snack and outside play activities if you include these items in your children's ministry.

When you see this icon, it means preparation will take more than five minutes.

TICKETS PLEASE!
(Welcome and Bible Connection)

■ **Objective:** *To excite children's interest and connect their own life experiences with the Bible Truth, children will play mini golf and discuss what it takes to win at a game.*

Welcome Time Activity: Mini Golf

■ **Materials:** *small golf-sized balls, cardboard wrapping paper tubes or toy hockey sticks/golf clubs, paper cups, masking tape*

As children arrive, send them to the mini golf site. Players take turns standing behind a masking tape line and use a cardboard tube or toy club to knock the ball into the cup. After their turn, they can go to the end of the line to try again. Players can take turns as ball gatherers to retrieve balls for those in line. Helpers can converse with children about the process of learning to play a game and get better so they win more often.

Sharing Time and Bible Connection

When everyone has arrived, call children to the lesson area and welcome them. As you move into the activity and discussion to prepare for the Bible story, give every child the opportunity to say something.

Ask children who played mini golf during the Welcome Time Activity how they did.

■ **What games do you like to play at home or school or in your neighborhood?**
■ **Why do you think you don't always win every time you play a game?** (because you're still learning, others are better players than you)
■ **How is playing a game like living life with God?** (you need to know God's rules, you need to practice, it doesn't always go the way you want, it can be hard, etc.)

This is our last week for learning about being winners in God's kingdom. You have all learned a lot and are growing in your skill of doing your best to honor God. Today's story is a parable Jesus told to show people what it means to be rich, but not with money. Let's find out what Jesus wanted us to understand.

ALL ABOARD FOR BIBLE TRUTH   Luke 12:16–21
(Bible Discover and Learn Time)

- ■ *Objective:* Children will study Luke 12:16–21 to discover how a rich man was foolish and ended up with nothing because he wasn't rich in character.
- ■ *Materials:* Bibles, building blocks

Set out blocks and ask students to work together to build a large building. Then they can sit down.

That's a good building you built. Let's pretend it's the building in this parable. Jesus told a story about a rich man. This man planted his fields, and one year everything in his field grew really well. He could see huge plants that were growing big and strong. The rich man was pretty pleased because he knew these crops would make him even richer.

When harvest time came, though, the man had a problem. "What am I going to do? I don't have enough barn space to store my big crop." How do you think the man could have used the extra grain God had given him? Discuss how he could have shared it with neighbors, the poor, and others.

Well, the rich man decided he would save every last bit of what he grew, so he tore down his nice barns and built bigger ones. Have the children knock down the block building and make a bigger one. **This man thought, "Pretty soon I'll have all the food and goods I'll ever need, and then I can just relax, have fun, and party."**

The rich man was just thinking of how to satisfy himself and get more money. He had to use all his time and energy for taking care of his stuff. What do you think God thought about that? (God wants us to care about his kingdom and live lives that serve others and honor him, not just create riches for ourselves)

The rich man wasn't interested in becoming more like Jesus. Instead, he made plans for his life on earth and thought only of himself.

What a terrible surprise came to the man. Soon after building bigger, better barns, God said to him, "You're a fool. Tonight, you're going to die. You won't get to keep even one thing you spent your whole life making. All your things will go to someone else." Knock down the building blocks. **The man was rich in stuff, but not in character. He didn't care about doing his best and winning in God's kingdom. And he lost his life and his stuff.**

After Jesus told this story to a group of people in Israel, he said, "That's why you should love God first and then love your neighbor. When you die, only what you have done for others and to serve God are of value."

The things God cares about are how we do our best to love and serve him and others. <u>Choosing to be a winner in God's eyes means we choose to be rich in things we won't lose.</u> We choose to be rich in our character, because we want to imitate Jesus. Even when we die here and go to heaven, we'll be winners.

Use the Clues!
(Bible Review)

■ *Materials: building blocks, ribbons (optional)*

Let's have fun reviewing our Bible story!

Tell the children they'll try to build a 'tower of character' by remembering the things they've learned about being winners. They can build individual, small group towers or one large group tower.

Review today's lesson and the past 12 weeks using *Use the Clues!* information in the Resources section. Ask children to name and describe the winner qualities shown on the ribbons on the winner's jersey. Each time they explain one quality, they can add a couple of blocks to their towers.

When the review is done, congratulate children by name for learning about and choosing to work at winning by becoming rich in their character. If you've decided to do so, give children winner ribbons.

BIBLE MEMORY WAYPOINT
(Scripture Memory)

Isaiah 40:31

■ *Objective: Children will hide God's Word in their hearts for guidance, protection, and encouragement.*

Those who hope in the LORD will renew their strength. They will soar on wings like eagles; they will run and not grow weary, they will walk and not be faint (Isaiah 40:31).

To help children memorize today's verse, read it aloud from the poster board, then read it with the children as you point to the words. Ask children to suggest actions that represent the words and ideas in the verse. As each action is chosen, recite the verse and add that action. Continue adding actions until there are several. Ask boys, then girls to perform the verse actions and say the verse, then recite one more time all together.

PRAYER STATION

- ■ *Objective: Children will explore and practice prayer for themselves in small groups.*
- ■ *Materials: copies of* StationMaster Card #13 *for each adult or teen helper*

Break into small groups of three to five children. Assign a teen or adult helper to each small group and give each helper a copy of *StationMaster Card #13* (see Resources) with ideas for group discussion and prayer.

SNACK STOP: WINNER'S REWARD (Optional)

If you plan to provide a snack, this is an ideal time to serve it.

- ■ *Materials: orange juice or sports drinks, fruit slices, cheese sticks or chunks, granola bars*

Choose any or all of the snack ideas, and allow children to choose a serving from your selection. Ask why these are foods athletes might eat (high protein, high energy, good nutrition). Remind children that as winners in God's kingdom, they also need daily servings of God's Word and time spent just with him.

Note: Always be aware of children with food allergies and have another option on hand if necessary.

APPLICATION

- ■ *Objective: Children will have opportunities to show how the lesson works in their own lives through activities and take-home papers.*

Some children's ministries may allow children to play outside at this point. If yours does not, choose one of the following activities.

Character Trophies

■ **Materials:** *medium- to large-size sturdy paper cups, 3" hard foam balls, craft or tempera paint in primary colors (red and/or blue are best), brushes, cardboard cut in 6" x 8" rectangles, gold and silver star stickers, glue and glue sticks, scissors, pins, colored construction paper*

Children can construct a trophy to signify their efforts at becoming winners in God's kingdom. Each will paint one hard foam ball and one cup. Push a pin through the center of the cup bottom from the inside, and place a couple of drops of glue on the pin where it emerges from the cup bottom exterior. Glue the cup upside down in the center of the cardboard. Impale the ball on the pin. Have each child write qualities of a winner on construction paper, cut them out, and glue them around the cup on the cardboard base. When the paint is dry on the cup, gold and silver star stickers can be applied.

Bible Story Review Bowling

■ **Materials:** *toy bowling set or 10 empty 2-liter bottles and a ball (one set per group)*

This game can be done as a single group or multiple groups depending on class size and room space. Set up the bowling pins/bottles. Children will line up and earn a chance to bowl by giving an example of a winner or Bible Truth from the past 13 weeks' Bible stories. Points can be kept as individuals or teams, as desired. Have two players at a time rotate through the job of resetting the bowling pins. To be able to bowl, ask each player to name one winner (Paul, Esther, Daniel, Samuel, Hannah, Elisha, Abigail, tax collector, Joseph, Mary, Martha, Rahab) or one Bible Truth (winners give their best, say yes to God's authority, act like winners, pay attention to God's voice, talk to God, use God's wisdom to make the best choices, are humble, follow God, care for those around them, choose to be truthful, put their faith into action).

ON THE FAST TRACK! *(Take-Home Papers)*

Let children who brought back a signed ticket from last week's take-home paper choose a prize from the treasure box. **This week is your last chance to do your *On the Fast Track!* paper for this lesson series. Don't forget to have a parent or guardian sign your ticket after you've completed the activities and learned your verse. Then bring it back next week to choose a prize from the treasure box!**

Distribute the take-home papers and trophies and winner ribbons, if made, just before children leave.

**Lesson 1
Tennis Shoes
Ribbon**

**Lesson 2
Scepter Ribbon**

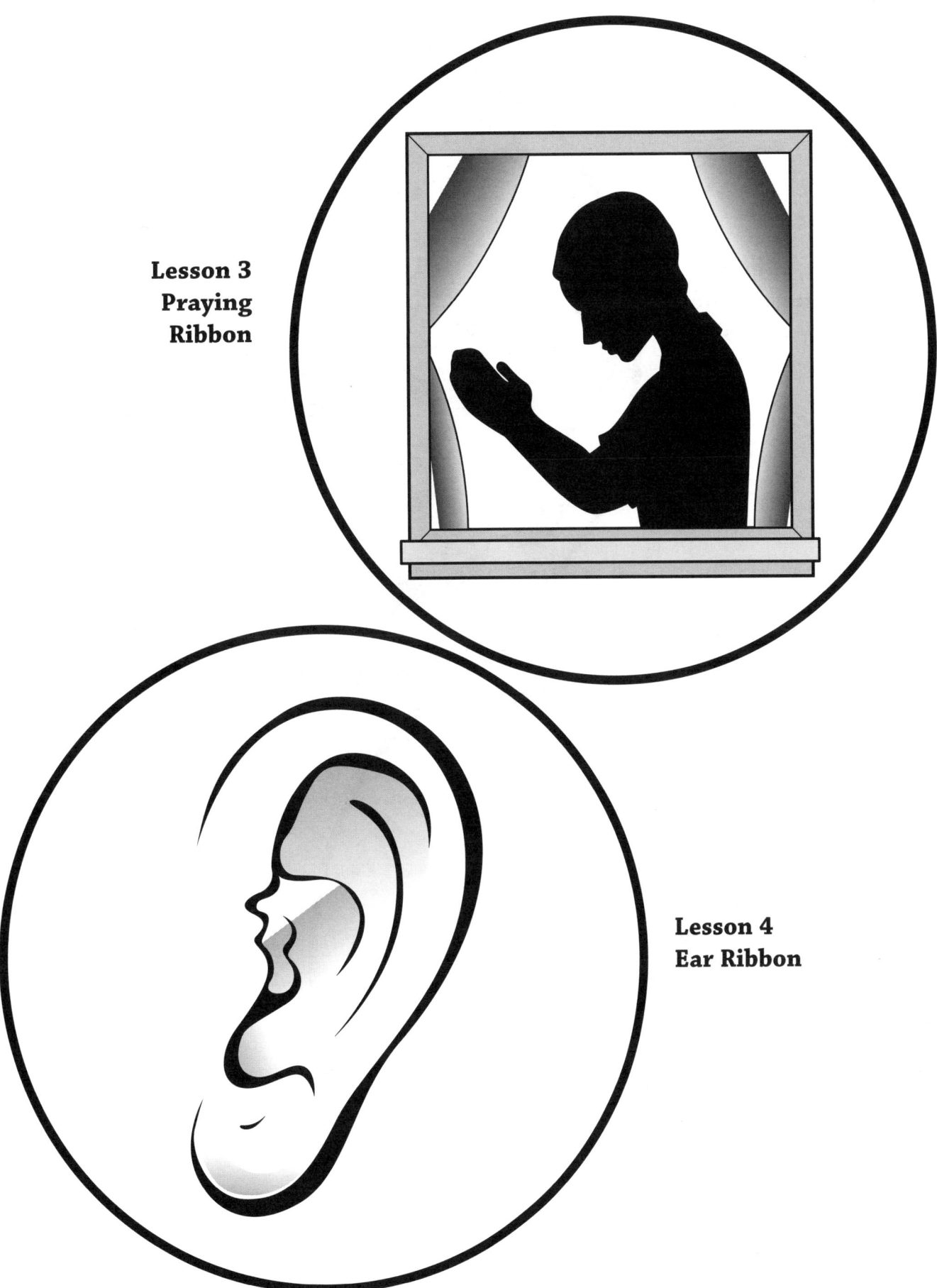

Lesson 3
Praying
Ribbon

Lesson 4
Ear Ribbon

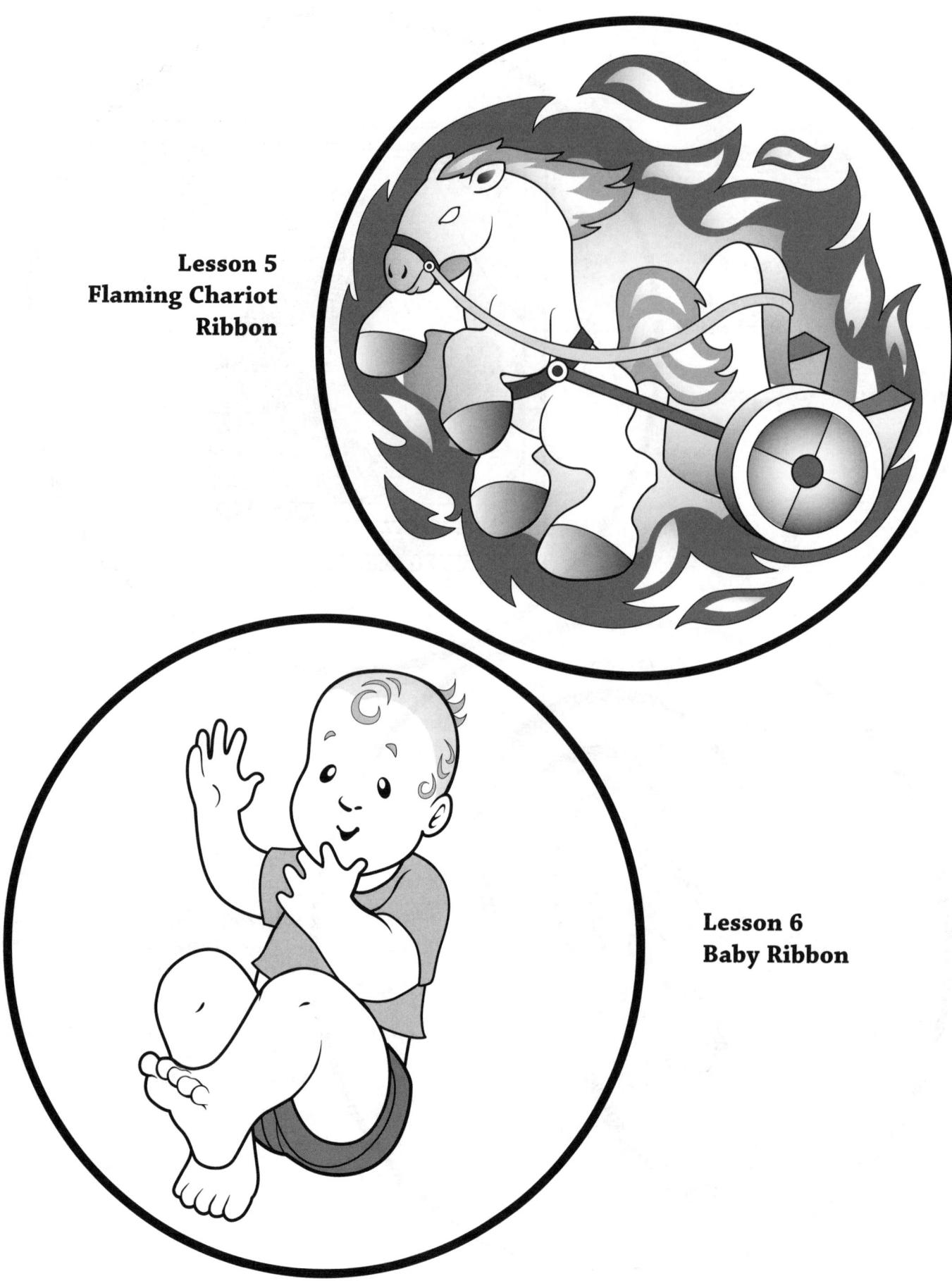

**Lesson 5
Flaming Chariot
Ribbon**

**Lesson 6
Baby Ribbon**

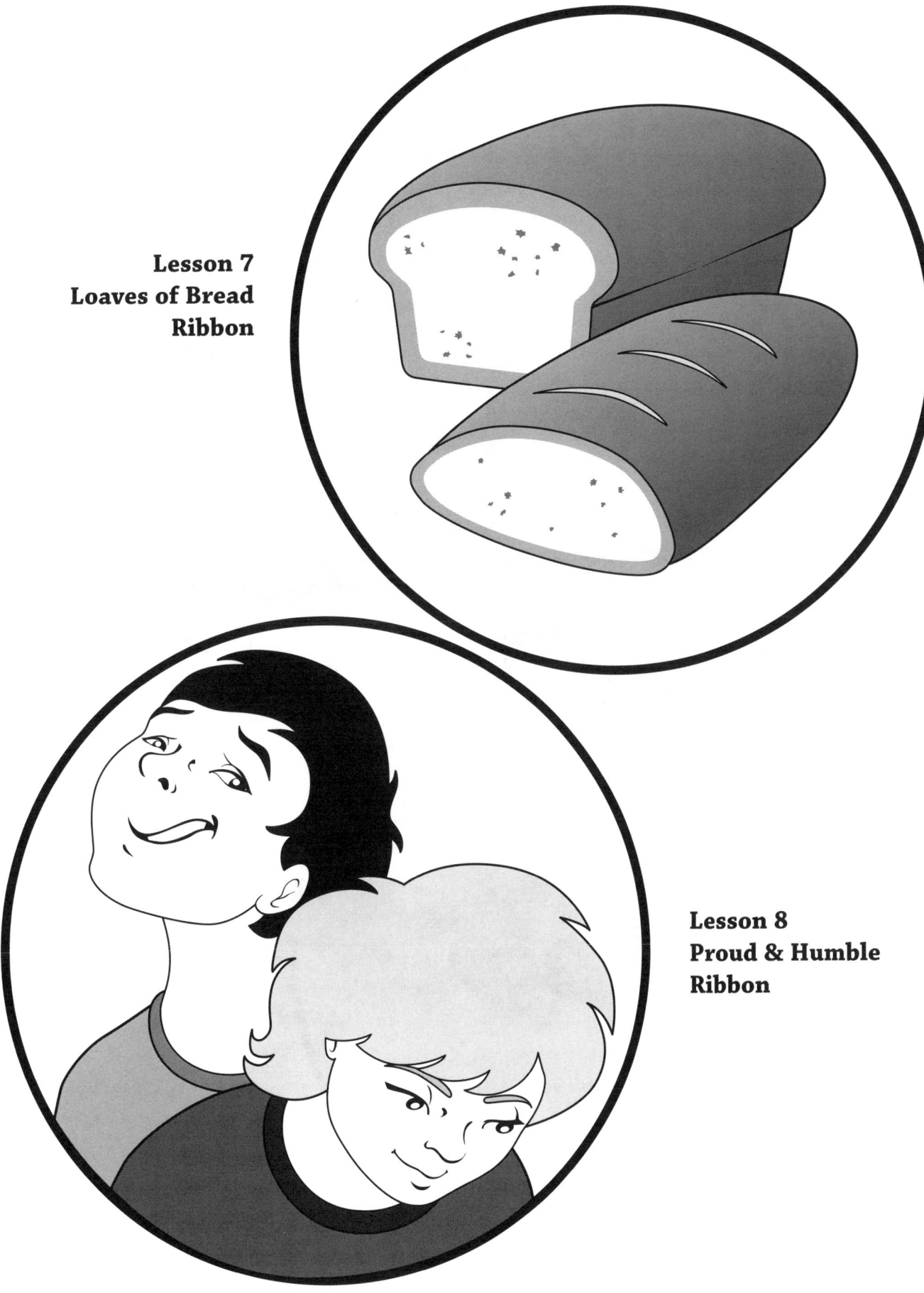

Lesson 7
Loaves of Bread
Ribbon

Lesson 8
Proud & Humble
Ribbon

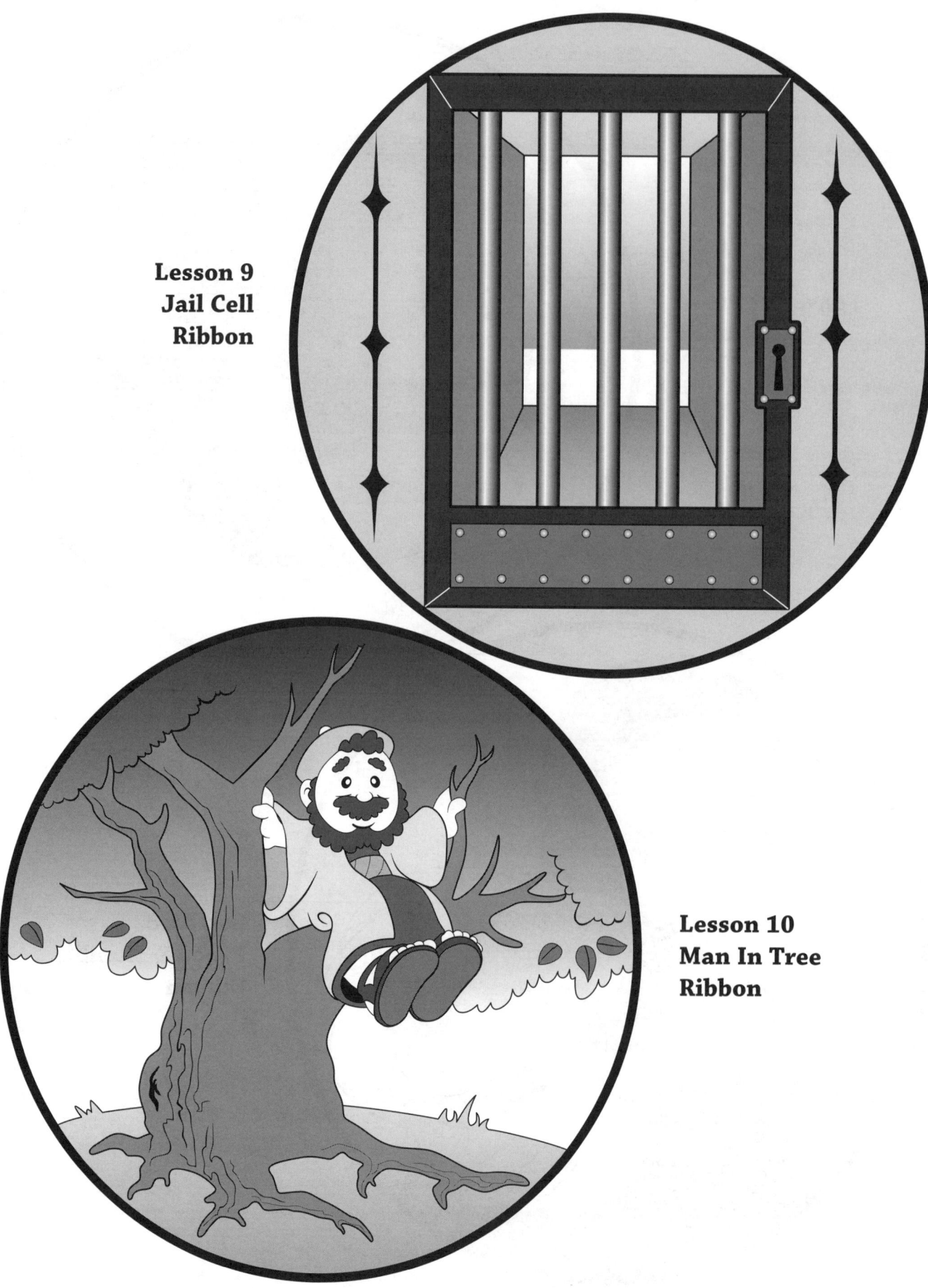

Lesson 9
Jail Cell
Ribbon

Lesson 10
Man In Tree
Ribbon

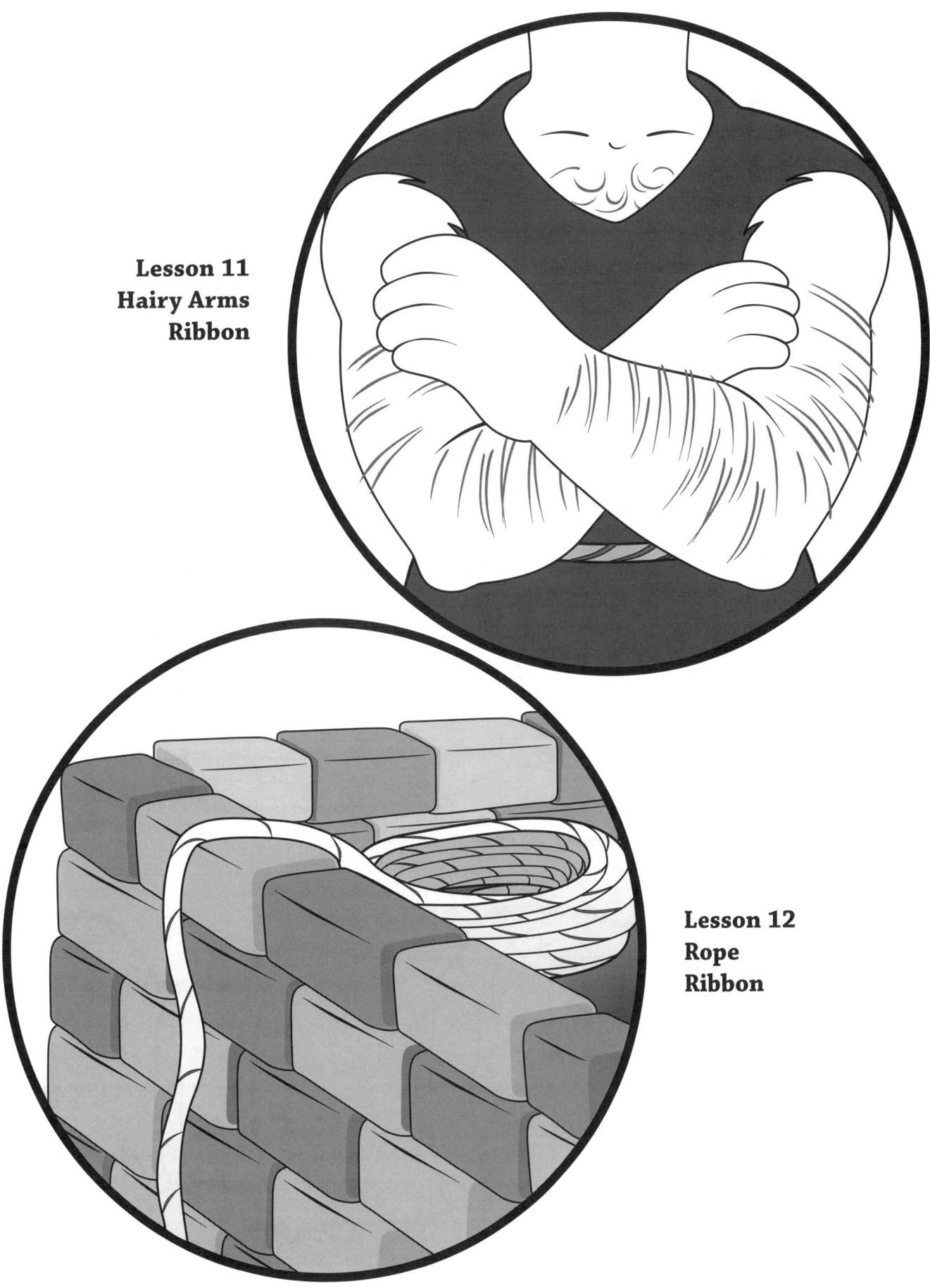

Lesson 11
Hairy Arms
Ribbon

Lesson 12
Rope
Ribbon

Lesson 12
Spy #1 Puppet

Lesson 12
Rahab Puppet

Lesson 12
Spy #2 Puppet

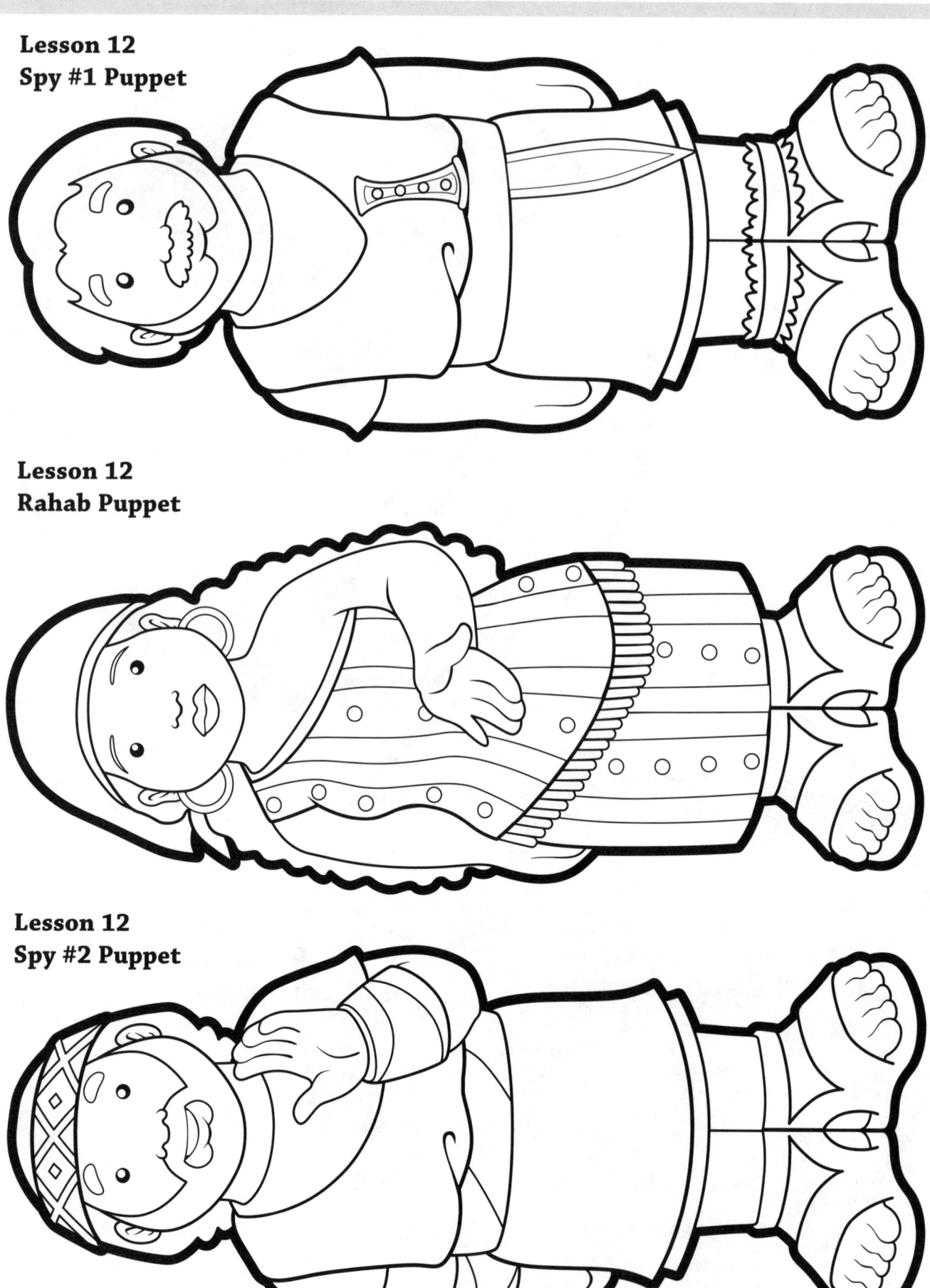

**Lesson 13
Winner Circle
Ribbon**

Bible Story Skit for Lesson 6

(Player slouches into the room holding a basketball or soccer ball.)

Coach: Hey, (name). I'm glad you showed up today. I was getting concerned you might not come. Have you warmed up?

Player: Warmed up? Were we supposed to do that? I didn't know!

Coach: Well, I would have told you if you had talked to me. But I didn't hear from you all week.

Player: Oh, well... *(starts frantically doing toe touches and jumping jacks)* Maybe I can catch up and be ready anyway.

Coach: Maybe. So what's that you're carrying?

Player: *(panting dramatically)* This soccer ball? I brought it for the game. It's always good to have a spare, you know.

Coach: You're right, but we aren't playing soccer today.

Player: *(stops, stunned)* We aren't playing soccer?

Coach: *(shakes head)* No, of course not.

Player: Then why did I bring my soccer ball?

Coach: That's what I was about to ask you! Why did you bring that ball?

Player: I thought we were playing soccer. I've been practicing ball handling and goal kicking, and even fancy footwork *(does some crazy hopping around)*. I'm ready to win today!

Coach: *(shaking head)* Oh, man. If you had talked to me, you wouldn't have used your time this week on soccer skills. Those won't do you any good.

Player: *(panicked)* Why? I thought I was going to be the starting forward for the team!

Coach: Nope, soccer season is over. We're starting basketball today. Are you ready to try out for the team?

Player: *(hangs head)* No way. I haven't worked on my basketball moves for a year. I goofed up big time.

Coach: And you could have been a winner, too. *(Shakes head and they walk away, coach's arm across player's shoulders.)*

Dear Parents,

During the next 13 weeks in children's ministry, your child will learn the value of obedience, the power of trusting God, and how to run the race of life with purpose. In our *And the Winner Is . . .* curriculum, kids will encounter Bible and modern-day heroes through exciting, interactive lessons. The children will also learn how to pray in small groups and will have opportunities to build lifetime habits of prayer.

And the Winner Is . . . uses the **imPACT** model of prayer to help children understand the four important activities of prayer—praise, ask, confess, and give thanks. Here are some discussion questions you may use at home to reinforce your child's growing desire to talk with God:

- *Praise.* Ask your child: **What do you really like about God?** Listen to the responses. Then say: **Let's tell God we like these things about him.** Encourage your child to tell God directly what he or she likes about him.

- *Ask.* It is important for children to know that God cares about their needs. We can ask God to help us, our families, and our friends with any problems. He wants everyone to ask him for what they need. **What would you like to ask God?** Let your child name some prayer requests. Then say: **Let's tell God about these needs.** Take turns praying for these needs.

- *Confess.* Tell your child that we all do things we wish we didn't do. Sometimes our actions or words hurt someone and then we are sorry. Ask: **What's one thing that you wish you didn't do this last week?** Listen to the response. Then say: **Let's confess our sin to God and tell him we're sorry.** Together, bow heads and confess this sin before God.

- *Give thanks.* Ask: **What are some things that you're thankful that God has done for you or has given to you?** Listen to the responses. Then say: **Let's tell God thank you for these things.** Take turns thanking God.

Real discipleship is such an important concept that your child will receive a take-home paper for each lesson, designed to support the Bible Truth for that day. These take-home papers will include fun activities, a Bible memory verse, and a prayer challenge. Some of the activities invite the involvement of the whole family. Encourage your child to complete these activities and bring the signed *Fast Track!* Ticket the following Sunday.

If you have any questions about this study, please feel free to discuss them with the children's ministry leaders. We are excited about what God is going to do in the lives of our children. We would appreciate your prayers for the teachers and children.

In His Name,

Children's Ministry Coordinator

Dear StationMaster,

Welcome to *Discipleship Junction!* During the next 13 weeks, you will play a major role in the lives of children as you pray with them in small groups. In the *And the Winner Is . . .* curriculum, your students will learn the value of obedience, the power of trusting God, and how to run the race of life with purpose. You will reinforce these lessons in discipleship even as you help build habits of prayer into their lives that will last a lifetime

The **imPACT** model of prayer will remind children about the four important activities of prayer: praise, ask, confess, and give thanks:

- *Praise.* Ask: **What do you really like about God?** Let volunteers briefly respond, then say: **Let's tell God we like these things about him.** Help children talk to God directly.

- *Ask.* Ask children: **What would you like to ask God?** Allow children to give prayer requests, then say: **Let's tell God about these needs.** It is important for children to know that God cares about everyone's needs. Have them take turns praying for the needs in their lives.

- *Confess.* We all do things we wish we didn't do. Sometimes our actions or words hurt someone and then we are sorry. Ask them: **What's one thing that you wish you didn't do this last week?** Give children time to answer, then say: **Let's confess our sins to God and tell him we're sorry.**

- *Give thanks.* When giving thanks, ask your group: **Tell one thing that you're thankful that God has done for you.** Let children share, then say: **Let's tell God thank you for these things.**

The children's ministry appreciates the important role that you have volunteered to fill. We are confident that God is going to do amazing things in the lives of our children.

Sincerely,

Children's Ministry Coordinator

 ## StationMaster Card #1

This week your group learned from 1 Corinthians 9 that *winners choose to give their best in the race of life.* They learned how Paul compared life to a race. Lead your group to pray using the imPACT model:

- *Praise.* **God has given us the bodies and minds he knew we would need for the race he wants us to run in our lives.** Have students praise God for specific features of their bodies and minds, like a good memory or perfect eyesight.

- *Ask.* **Paul gave his best to running the race of life and winning.** Have students ask God to help them give their best, to be disciplined and focused on him.

- *Confess.* **It's not easy to keep running when we get mad or stubborn or sad. This is a** **chance to tell God you're sorry for a time you've had an attitude of quitting or been frustrated about doing things God's way.** Allow time for silent confession.

- *Thank.* **Paul was excited to run his race of life and reach the finish line. Let's each thank God for giving us energy today to keep going and friends to encourage us along the way.** Model a sentence prayer of specific thanks, then let students pray.

Remember that no child should be forced to pray, but do encourage and invite each one to join you. After "Amen," talk quietly to the children in your group until the next activity.

StationMaster Card #2

This week your group learned from Esther 4 and 5 that *winners say yes to God's authority.* They heard how Esther saved the Jewish people by submitting to God's authority. Lead your group in these four activities of prayer:

■ *Praise.* **God saved his chosen people, the Jews, from death by using Esther's obedience to him.** Lead students in praising God for using each of us for his greater plan.

■ *Ask.* **Being under authority can be hard when you want to do something different than what you are asked to do.** Students can ask God to help them submit a particular area of their lives to him.

■ *Confess.* **Esther was scared to go in to the king**

of Persia without an invitation. **Have you ever been afraid to do the right thing? Let's each tell God we're sorry for sometimes being too scared to do what's right. We can be sure God will forgive us.**

■ *Thank.* **Lots of times we ask God for help and after he helps us, we forget to thank him. Now is a chance to thank God for what he's done for you this week.** Allow students to pray as they choose.

Remember that no child should be forced to pray, but do encourage and invite each one to join you. After "Amen," talk quietly to the children in your group until the next activity.

StationMaster Card #3

This week your group learned from Daniel 6 that *winners act like winners in all they do.* The Bible story taught that Daniel didn't stop honoring God even when it was against the law, and thus he was a winner in God's kingdom. Lead your group in these four activities of prayer:

■ *Praise.* **We saw in the Bible story that God knows how to turn bad situations into something good.** Have students praise God for individual or general ways God uses all things for his purposes.

■ *Ask.* **Daniel continued to pray even when he knew that others had plotted against him.** Lead students in asking God for the strength and courage to follow him even when it's not the

popular thing to do.

■ *Confess.* **It's not easy sometimes to be a winner with strong spiritual character. We all make mistakes.** Students can ask God for forgiveness for times when they haven't acted like they know God would want them to act.

■ *Thank.* **Daniel did what God wanted him to do, no matter the consequences.** Have students thank God for being there even in hard times.

Remember that no child should be forced to pray, but do encourage and invite each one to join you. After "Amen," talk quietly to the children in your group until the next activity.

StationMaster Card #4

This week your group learned from 1 Samuel 3 that *winners pay attention to God's voice.* They discovered that Samuel learned to recognize God's voice and was a winner because he paid attention when God spoke to him. Lead your group in these four activities of prayer:

- *Praise.* **God spoke to Samuel.** Lead students in praising God for knowing their names and everything about them.
- *Ask.* **Samuel was ready to hear from God. Are you ready?** Pray with students, asking that they will know God's voice when he wants their attention.
- *Confess.* **When we don't like the message or are busy with our own things, we sometimes choose not to pay attention.** Give students opportunity to confess to God times they haven't paid attention to adults or to him.
- *Thank.* **It's amazing that the God who created everything in the world wants to walk with us and be part of our lives. Let's thank God for caring about us and knowing what's best for us.**

Remember that no child should be forced to pray, but do encourage and invite each one to join you. After "Amen," talk quietly to the children in your group until the next activity.

StationMaster Card #5

This week your group learned from 2 Kings 6 that *winners trust God.* They learned that Elisha trusted God and how important it is for us to know that God is in control, no matter what the situation looks like. Lead your group in these four activities of prayer:

- *Praise.* **Elisha saw God's heavenly army ready to fight for him.** Have students praise God for always being with them and being in control of the situations they are in.
- *Ask.* **Sometimes we aren't happy with our situation and forget that God has put us there. When we're worried or unhappy, God wants us to ask him to give us spiritual eyes to see things the way He does.** Lead students in asking God for spiritual eyes and greater trust in any situation.
- *Confess.* **Elisha prayed that his servant's eyes would be opened so his servant would stop worrying. When have you worried instead of trusting God?** Have students ask God for forgiveness for worrying. Provide an example by being specific in your own sentence prayer.
- *Thank.* **Even when we can't see what God has in store, we can be sure God is in control of every situation, just like Elisha was sure.** Model a prayer of thanks to God for teaching you how to trust him no matter what.

Remember that no child should be forced to pray, but do encourage and invite each one to join you. After "Amen," talk quietly to the children in your group until the next activity.

StationMaster Card #6

This week your group learned from 1 Samuel 1 that *winners talk to God*. They discovered that Hannah talked to God and had a close relationship with Him. Lead your group in these four activities of prayer:

- *Praise.* **God desires to have us really know him and talk to him a lot.** Lead students in praising God for his unfathomable love for them.
- *Ask.* **When we don't know what to say to God, we can just tell him that, and ask His help in knowing how to pray. God understands.** Have students ask God to teach them how to pray.
- *Confess.* **Have you ever not wanted to talk to God? That happens, but we can tell God we're sorry for ignoring him or choosing to** do something else rather than pray. Model for students a prayer asking forgiveness for not choosing to talk to God.
- *Thank.* **It's hard to imagine how, but God can hear us whenever we talk to him, no matter how many other people may be praying at the same time!** Students can thank God for his ability to listen to them anytime and anywhere.

Remember that no child should be forced to pray, but do encourage and invite each one to join you. After "Amen," talk quietly to the children in your group until the next activity.

StationMaster Card #7

This week your group learned from 1 Samuel 25 that *winners use God's wisdom to make the best choices*. They saw how Abigail saved herself and her household by using God's sound judgment. Lead your group in these four activities of prayer:

- *Praise.* **God has given us many examples in the Bible of people who searched out his wisdom. Let's praise him for being wise in all things.**
- *Ask.* **God says we should ask for wisdom, and he will be glad to give it. Think of one thing you need godly wisdom for.** Encourage students to pray specifically for wisdom in a particular circumstance.
- *Confess.* **Not all of our choices are good ones. Can you think of a choice recently that you know wasn't the best one? Take this time to tell God you're sorry for making that choice.**
- Thank. **Abigail was rewarded for showing godly wisdom. How has God blessed or helped you through his wise care?** Lead students in a time of thanksgiving to the Lord for how he wisely leads and cares for them. Let them pray specifically or generally.

Remember that no child should be forced to pray, but do encourage and invite each one to join you. After "Amen," talk quietly to the children in your group until the next activity.

StationMaster Card #8

This week your group learned from Luke 18 that *winners are humble, not proud.* They learned how a tax collector's prayer showed humility compared to the proud, self-righteous prayer of a Pharisee. Lead your group in these four activities of prayer:

- ■ *Praise.* **One thing we can never do too much of is praise God, sincerely and from our hearts. Let's praise him right now for loving us no matter how proud we can sometimes act.** Lead students in praising God in short phrases and sentences.
- ■ *Ask.* **The only way to begin learning to be humble, not proud, is to ask God to teach us.** Model for students how to ask for a humble heart and attitude, and let children follow your example as they choose.

- ■ *Confess.* **For a minute, be quiet and let God bring to your mind ways you've been proud. Then ask his forgiveness for that.** After a silent minute, lead students in prayers of confession.
- ■ *Thank.* **Aren't you glad God sees into your heart and knows when you're choosing to behave humbly instead of proudly? Let's thank God for knowing us from the inside out, and helping us grow to be more like Jesus.** Allow students to freely thank God.

Remember that no child should be forced to pray, but do encourage and invite each one. After "Amen," talk quietly to the children in your group until the next activity.

StationMaster Card #9

This week your group learned from Genesis 37, 39—41 that *winners follow God no matter what.* They learned how God released Joseph from prison and put him in charge of Egypt. Lead your group in these four activities of prayer:

- ■ *Praise.* **Joseph went from prison to being made the second in charge of all of Egypt.** Have students praise God for being able to overcome any situation or problem.
- ■ *Ask.* **Joseph trusted in God when things were going well and God helped him keep going in hard times.** Have students ask God to remind them that he is leading them even when life isn't going well.
- ■ *Confess.* **Joseph didn't complain even when**

one bad thing after another happened to him. Most of us complain often, even if it's not out loud. Let's ask God to forgive us for complaining instead of trusting in him.
- ■ *Thank.* **Maybe God has already led you through a hard time. This is a chance to thank him for being there with you. If you haven't had those hard times, thank God that you can depend on him in both good and bad situations.** Lead children in genuine thanksgiving to God.

Remember that no child should be forced to pray, but do encourage and invite each one to join you. After "Amen," talk quietly to the children in your group until the next activity.

StationMaster Card #10

This week your group learned from Luke 19 that *winners care for those around them*. They discovered how Jesus showed care for Zacchaeus. Lead your group in these four activities of prayer:

■ *Praise.* **God has put lots of people in our lives to show care for us.** Have students praise God for caring about their needs.

■ *Ask.* **We sometimes don't see the ways we can care for someone.** Lead students in asking God to open their eyes to who they can care for in their daily lives.

■ *Confess.* **Sometimes we're selfish and don't** want to care about another person. Instead, we want them to do something for us. Allow students to ask forgiveness for times of selfishness and ignoring others' needs.

■ *Thank.* **We can care for other people because God takes such great care of us.** Let students consider specific ways they're thankful for God's care, and then express that thanks one by one.

Remember that no child should be forced to pray, but do encourage and invite each one to join you. After "Amen," talk quietly to the children in your group until the next activity.

StationMaster Card #11

This week your group learned from Genesis 27 and 33 that *winners choose to be truthful*. They learned how Jacob and Rebekah lied to Isaac and deceived him, and their family was torn apart as a result. Lead your group in these four activities of prayer:

■ *Praise.* **No matter how we might get into trouble by not being truthful, God never lies to us. He is totally the Truth.** Have students praise God as the Way, the Truth, and the Life.

■ *Ask.* **God will always help us become more truthful. All we need to do is ask him and do our best to choose the truth.** Have students ask God for the courage to always tell the truth.

■ *Confess.* **Even when we don't choose to be** truthful, we can ask God for forgiveness and start over. Give students the opportunity to confess any untruthful experiences.

■ *Thank.* **Don't you feel relieved and free when God has forgiven you? He's so ready to clean us up after our sin. Let's give God thanks for being so willing to take away our sinfulness.** Lead students in sentence prayers of thanksgiving.

Remember that no child should be forced to pray, but do encourage and invite each one to join you. After "Amen," talk quietly to the children in your group until the next activity.

StationMaster Card #12

This week your group learned from Joshua 2 and 6 that *winners put their faith into action.* They learned how Rahab helped the Israelite spies. Lead your group in these four activities of prayer:

- *Praise.* **Rahab believed in the God of Israel.** Have students praise God for being amazing, miracle-working, caring, and protective.
- *Ask.* **Rahab asked the spies to protect her when the city was destroyed. God wants us to ask him for his help too.** Encourage students to ask God's help with specific situations in their lives.
- *Confess.* **Rahab risked her life to save the Israelite spies. She put her faith into action.**

We sometimes hang back and don't act when we should. Give students opportunity to confess when they have chosen not to act, but know they should have.

- *Thank.* **Do you think Rahab was grateful she was saved from death in Jericho? Like Rahab, God has done things for us that we should be thankful for. Let's thank God now for how we have felt or seen his care and help this week.**

Remember that no child should be forced to pray, but do encourage and invite each one to join you. After "Amen," talk quietly to the children in your group until the next activity.

StationMaster Card #13

This week your group learned from Luke 12 that *winners know the real prize is being rich in character.* They discovered how a rich man ended up with nothing because he didn't care about winning for God's kingdom. Lead your group in these four activities of prayer:

- *Praise.* **God is the perfect example to us of good character.** Have students praise him for specific attributes of who he is.
- *Ask.* **The rich man is our example of how NOT to live. Let's ask God to build in us character qualities that we've learned about these past 13 weeks.** Lead students in asking God to help them grow stronger in one of the qualities studied.

- *Confess.* **Do you think God would have forgiven the rich man if he had realized his mistake and repented? Of course! And God is willing to forgive you and me when we do wrong or ignore his ways.** Encourage children to search their hearts and confess sin.
- *Thank.* **Not only does God totally forgive us when we sincerely ask, he also works with us to keep us going along his way. Take a minute to thank God for one thing you have learned or he has done in your life this week.**

Remember that no child should be forced to pray, but do encourage and invite each one to join you. After "Amen," talk quietly to the children in your group until the next activity.

On the Fast Track!

And the Winner Is...

Paul

Bible Memory Verse

I consider everything a loss compared to the surpassing greatness of **knowing Christ Jesus my Lord,** for whose sake I have lost all things. I consider them rubbish, that I may gain Christ **(Philippians 3:8).** *Early elementary verse in **bold** type.*

Word Search

Find these hidden words in the word search below.

BEST GREAT KINGDOM LIFE PAUL
PRIZE RACE RUBBISH RUNNER

J	D	R	O	R	G	K	Q	V	L	C	P
A	A	U	T	U	U	B	E	S	T	R	L
O	D	N	L	P	H	B	M	A	I	L	U
K	I	N	G	D	O	M	B	Z	N	W	A
H	Q	E	C	Z	K	Y	E	I	M	H	P
N	A	R	M	T	W	Y	E	T	S	D	M
B	B	O	E	K	Z	H	Z	C	Y	H	B
H	K	F	O	T	A	E	R	G	A	V	H
W	I	L	X	E	Y	Z	B	P	O	R	W
L	M	Q	W	Y	L	H	K	X	C	Z	Q
S	O	E	N	P	E	O	S	E	G	G	M
V	Q	E	J	I	C	D	S	U	K	O	V

Trading Cards

Add some color to the trading card of Paul and write at the bottom: Winners give their best. Cut out the card and put it in an envelope or other safe place. You're going to be making a whole collection over the next 13 weeks!

Prayer Challenge

This week we learned about how Paul saw life as a race. He knew that it takes hard work and good self-control to run well. Think about an area of your life where you need better self-control or more discipline. Ask God to help you so you can be a winner for his kingdom!

Dear Parents and Guardians,

Please check off the items your child completed this week:

- ☐ Prayer Challenge
- ☐ Memory Verse
- ☐ Paul Trading Card
- ☐ Word Search

Adult Signature: _____

FAST TRACK! TICKET

On the Fast Track!

And the Winner Is...

Esther

Trading Cards

Add some color to the trading card of Esther and write at the bottom: A winner says yes to God's authority. Cut out the card and add it to last week's to build your collection!

Bible Memory Verse

And we know that **in all things God works for the good of those who love him,** who have been called according to his purpose **(Romans 8:28)**. *Early elementary verse in **bold** type.*

Prayer Challenge

Remember how Esther obeyed God's authority and respected the king whom God had placed over her? Use your trading cards as bookmarks in your schoolbooks this week. Every time you see your cards, say a sentence prayer for your teacher. Remember that God wants you to obey your teacher who has authority over you. Tell a parent or another adult one way you respected your teacher's authority this week.

Acrostic

For each letter below, write a word that begins with that letter and has to do with authority. You can list people who have authority over you, words that describe authority, or anything that makes you think of authority.

A _____

U _____

T _____

H _____

O _____

R _____

I _____

T _____

Y _____

Dear Parents and Guardians, *Please check off the items your child completed this week:*

- ❏ Prayer Challenge
- ❏ Memory Verse
- ❏ Esther Trading Card
- ❏ Acrostic

Adult Signature: _____

FAST TRACK! TICKET

On the Fast Track!

Bible Memory Verse

Even a child is known by his actions, by whether his conduct is pure and right (Proverbs 20:11).

Prayer Challenge

Think about one thing or place where you have a hard time acting the way you know God wants you to act. Then do what Daniel did. At least one time a day, for the whole week, kneel in your room and tell God you really want to act like a winner in this certain situation.

Crossword Puzzle

Look up the verses below to discover the answers for the puzzle.

- Daniel 6:4 They could find no corruption in [Daniel] because he was (1-down) _____.
- Daniel 6:7 Anyone who prays to any god or man during the next _____ (1–across)days ... shall be thrown into the lion's den.
- Daniel 6:10 [Daniel] went to his _____ (2-across) room.
- Daniel 6:10 Three times a day he got down on his knees and _____ (3-down).
- Daniel 6:16 The king said, "May your God whom you serve _____ (6-across), rescue you!"
- Daniel 6:22 My God sent his _____ (4-down) and he shut the mouths of the _____ (5-down).

Trading Cards

Add some color to the trading card of Daniel and write at the bottom: Winners act like winners in all they do. Cut out the card and add it to last week's to build your collection!

And the Winner Is...

Daniel

Dear Parents and Guardians,

Please check off the items your child completed this week:

- ☐ Prayer Challenge
- ☐ Memory Verse
- ☐ Daniel Trading Card
- ☐ Crossword Puzzle

Adult Signature:

_____

FAST TRACK! TICKET

And the Winner Is...

Samuel

Trading Cards

Add some color to the trading card of Samuel and write at the bottom: Winners pay attention to God's voice. Cut out the card and add it to last week's to build your collection!

Bible Memory Verse

My sheep listen to my voice; I know them, and they follow me (John 10:27).

Prayer Challenge

This week we learned about Samuel and how well he listened to God's voice. Find a quiet place and read a verse from Psalm 111 in your Bible. Then close your eyes and listen. Read another verse and listen again. Do this with a parent or other adult if you'd like and talk about what God is telling you. Remember, you may not hear God's voice out loud but know that God is with you and will give you thoughts through his Word.

Think and Do

Choose some worship music that you like and listen to it sometime this week. As you listen, create a drawing or a painting that shows how you feel about God as your shepherd. Have fun being creative! Bring the picture with you next week when you return your *Fast Track!* Ticket.

Dear Parents and Guardians,

Please check off the items your child completed this week:

❑ Prayer Challenge
❑ Memory Verse
❑ Samuel Trading Card
❑ Think and Do

Adult Signature: _____

FAST TRACK! TICKET

On the Fast Track!

Bible Memory Verse

Trust in the LORD with all your heart and lean not on your own understanding; in all your ways acknowledge him **and he will make your paths straight (Proverbs 3:5–6).**

Early elementary verse in **bold** *type.*

Trading Cards

Add some color to the trading card of Elisha and write at the bottom: Winners trust God. Cut out the card and add it to last week's to build your collection!

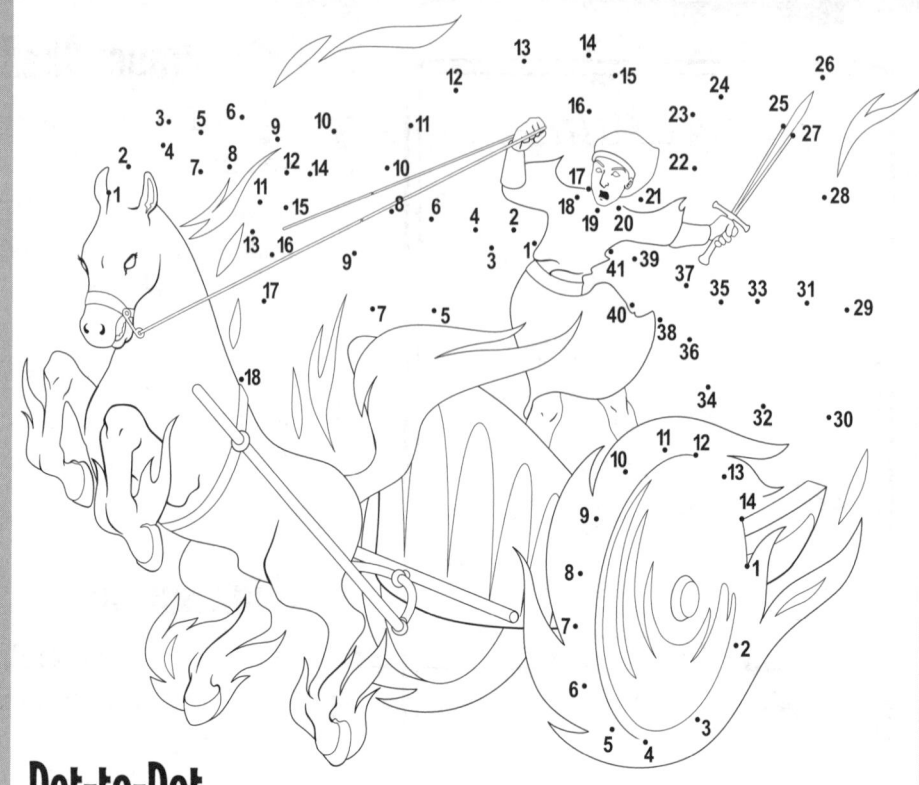

Dot-to-Dot

Connect the dots to find an image that will help remind you to trust God.

And the Winner Is...

Elisha

Prayer Challenge

In this week's lesson, Elisha trusted God because he saw with spiritual eyes. Learning to trust God no matter what isn't easy. Praying for God to change your feelings can make a big difference. This week, when you are unhappy or worried, tell God how you feel. Ask him to help you trust him in everything. At the end of the week, see how your spiritual eyes are seeing a little differently.

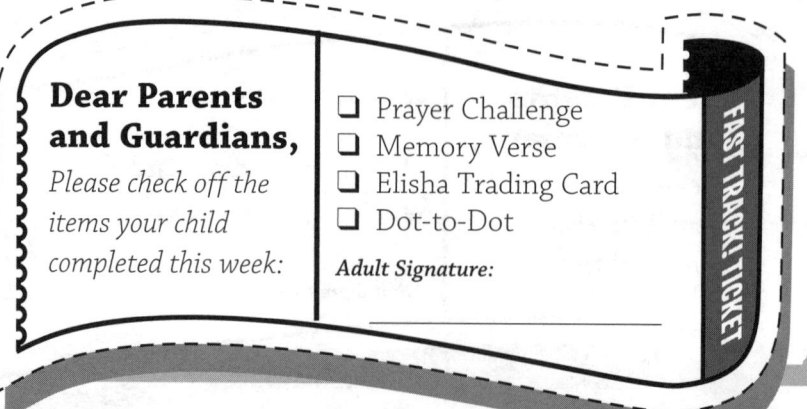

Dear Parents and Guardians,

Please check off the items your child completed this week:

❑ Prayer Challenge
❑ Memory Verse
❑ Elisha Trading Card
❑ Dot-to-Dot

Adult Signature:

FAST TRACK! TICKET

On the Fast Track!

And the Winner Is...

Hannah

Trading Cards

Add some color to the trading card of Hannah and write at the bottom: Winners talk to God. Cut out the card and add it to last week's to build your collection!

Bible Memory Verse

Give thanks to the LORD, call on his name; make known among the nations what he has done (Psalm 105:1).

Prayer Challenge

Remember how Hannah talked to God in this week's lesson? Every day this week, talk to God in a different way. You can pray by yourself and then with your parents, friends, siblings, or others. Talk to him in your bedroom, kitchen, living room, and car. Remember that God is with you everywhere and always wants you to talk to him!

Code For...

Finish the sentence by using the code below.
I love those who...

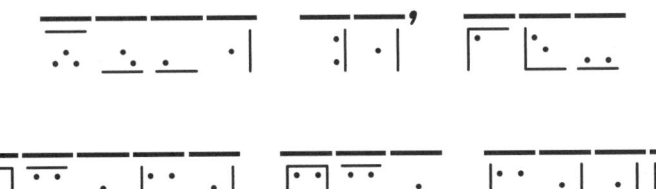

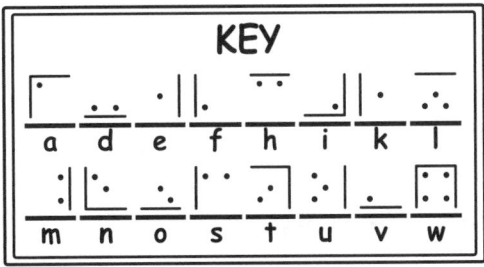

KEY

a d e f h i k l
m n o s t u v w

Dear Parents and Guardians,

Please check off the items your child completed this week:

❑ Prayer Challenge
❑ Memory Verse
❑ Hannah Trading Card
❑ Code For...

Adult Signature: _____

FAST TRACK! TICKET

On the Fast Track!

And the Winner Is...

Abigail

Trading Cards

Add some color to the trading card of Abigail and write at the bottom: Winners use God's wisdom to make the best choices. Cut out the card and add it to last week's to build your collection!

Bible Memory Verse

If any of you lacks wisdom, he should ask God, who gives generously to all without finding fault, **and it will be given to him (James 1:5).**

*Early elementary verse in **bold** type.*

Prayer Challenge

This week we learned about how Abigail used God's wisdom and saved her whole household from being killed. You can use God's wisdom too! Cut a piece of paper into six sections. Write these words on different pieces: friends, home, school, play, TV/computer, using time. Pull out a different slip each day. Ask God to give you wisdom to make good choices about the topic on the paper. At the end of the week, talk with an adult about how God has been showing you his wisdom in your life.

Think and Do

With a parent or other adult, read Proverbs 3. It might take a couple of days to read the whole chapter. Make a poster for your room that reminds you what Proverbs 3 says about wisdom. You can draw symbols, pictures that show a situation where you used wisdom, fancy lettered words, or whatever you choose.

WISDOM

Dear Parents and Guardians,
Please check off the items your child completed this week:

- ❏ Prayer Challenge
- ❏ Memory Verse
- ❏ Abigail Trading Card
- ❏ Think and Do

Adult Signature: _____

FAST TRACK! TICKET

And the Winner Is...

Tax Collector

Trading Cards

Add some color to the trading card of the tax collector and write at the bottom: Winners are humble, not proud. Cut out the card and add it to last week's to build your collection!

Bible Memory Verse

Do nothing out of selfish ambition or vain conceit, but in humility consider others better than yourselves. Each of you should look not only to your own interests, but also to the interests of others **(Philippians 2:3-4)**.

Early elementary verse in **bold** *type.*

Prayer Challenge

Remember what the tax collector said to God in this week's lesson? He said, "Lord, be merciful to me, because I'm a sinner." This week when you pray, start with those same words. God is glad to forgive your sins when you are humble enough to admit what you did wrong.

Word Scramble

Unscramble the words to discover how to pop the pride bubbles. (For the answer, see Titus 3:2.)

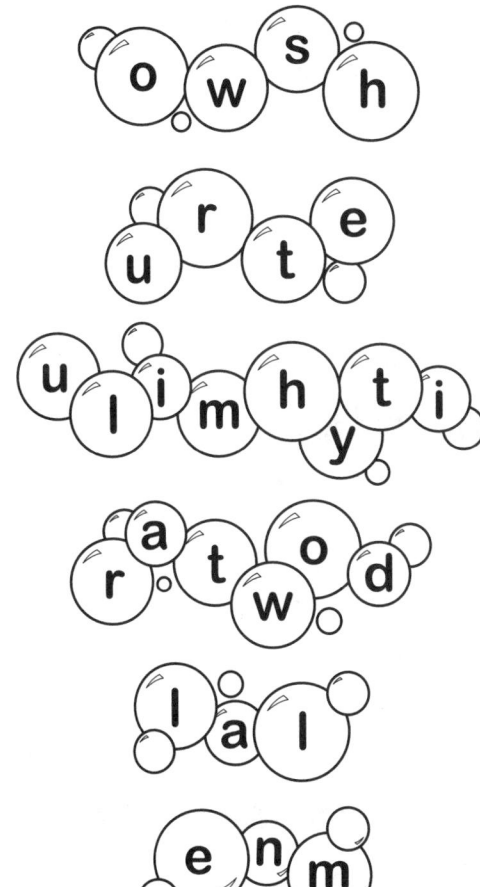

Dear Parents and Guardians,

Please check off the items your child completed this week:

❑ Prayer Challenge
❑ Memory Verse
❑ Tax Collector Trading Card
❑ Word Scramble

Adult Signature: _____

FAST TRACK! TICKET

And the Winner Is...

Joseph

Trading Cards

Add some color to the trading card of Joseph and write at the bottom: Winners follow God no matter what. Cut out the card and add it to last week's to build your collection!

Bible Memory Verse

The LORD himself goes before you and will be with you; he **will never leave** you nor forsake you. **Do not be afraid; do not be discouraged** (Deuteronomy 31:8). *Early elementary verse in* **bold** *type.*

Prayer Challenge

In this week's lesson, Joseph followed God even when bad things happened to him. But God had a good plan for Joseph, didn't he? For this week's prayer challenge, pray every day for five days. Each day, thank God that he goes before you and is with you, like your memory verse says. Then pray for God to lead you in your day. When you need to make a choice or are in a hard situation, ask God to help you. At the end of the week, look back and see how God has done this!

Maze

Draw a line to help this child follow Jesus no matter what.

START

END

Dear Parents and Guardians,
Please check off the items your child completed this week:

- ☐ Prayer Challenge
- ☐ Memory Verse
- ☐ Joseph Trading Card
- ☐ Maze

Adult Signature: _____

FAST TRACK! TICKET

And the Winner Is...

Jesus

Trading Cards

Add some color to the trading card of Jesus and write at the bottom: Winners care for those around them. Cut out the card and add it to last week's to build your collection!

 ## Bible Memory Verse

Serve wholeheartedly, as if you were serving the Lord, not men (Ephesians 6:7).

 ## Prayer Challenge

This week we saw how Jesus cared for a person that everyone else disliked. Think of one person in your life that you know is lonely or hurting. Pray for that person every day for five days this week.

Think and Do

Look around you to see the needs of your neighbors and friends. Is someone sick? If so, make her a card or some chicken soup. Is someone sad? Write him a letter, draw him a picture, or visit. Does someone in your family need help? Clear the table, walk the dog, or maybe offer to do an extra chore. By the end of the week, share with your parents what you have done to show care to others.

Dear Parents and Guardians,

Please check off the items your child completed this week:

- ☐ Prayer Challenge
- ☐ Memory Verse
- ☐ Jesus Trading Card
- ☐ Think and Do

Adult Signature: _____

FAST TRACK! TICKET

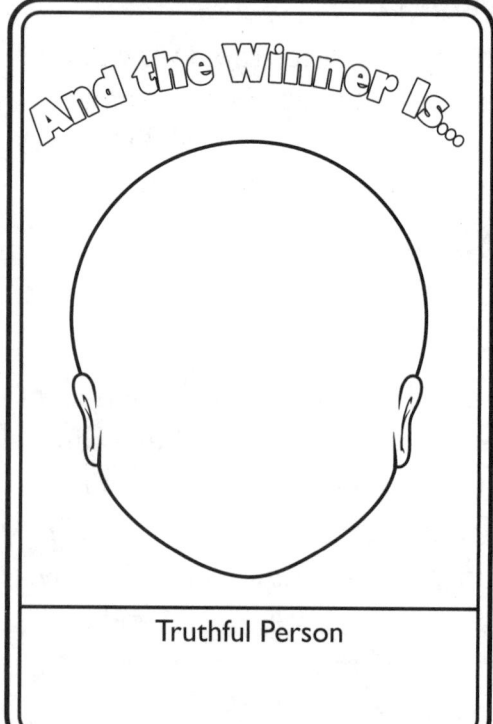

On the Fast Track!

And the Winner Is...

Truthful Person

Prayer Challenge

No one in this week's lesson acted like a winner, did they? Jacob and Rebekah lied and Esau wanted to kill Jacob. God wants us to be truthful all of the time so we can be winners. When you talk to God each day, remember that he already knows everything about you. Because he loves you, he wants you to tell him the truth. So, this week, make sure you practice telling the whole truth about everything.

Trading Cards

On the trading card for this week, draw in the face of someone you know who has been truthful recently. Add some color to the card and write at the bottom: Winners choose to be truthful. Cut out the card and add it to last week's to build your collection!

Think and Do

Play "I Spy" with a parent, other adult, or friend. Look and listen for lies on TV shows, movies, the radio, on the Internet, and in what you read. Each time you spot a lie—even the tiniest one— tell God you choose only to be truthful.

TRUTH

Bible Memory Verse

Love does not delight in evil but rejoices with the truth (1 Corinthians 13:6).

Dear Parents and Guardians,

Please check off the items your child completed this week:

- ☐ Prayer Challenge
- ☐ Memory Verse
- ☐ Truthful Person Trading Card
- ☐ Think and Do

Adult Signature: _____

FAST TRACK! TICKET

And the Winner Is...

Rahab

Trading Cards

Add some color to the trading card of Rahab and write at the bottom: Winners put their faith into action. Add this trading card to last week's to build your collection!

Prayer Challenge

Rahab showed her faith by helping God's people in this week's lesson. Getting started can be the hardest part of using your faith. So ask God to show you ways to put your faith into action. Pray this every day, and then look for his answer.

Think and Do

This week wear something red every day. It can be clothes, shoes, jewelry, a piece of yarn tied around your wrist, or a hat. The red will remind you of how Rahab acted on her faith. Expect God to show you how to act on your faith. When he does show you and you act in faith, tell someone at home or at church what happened.

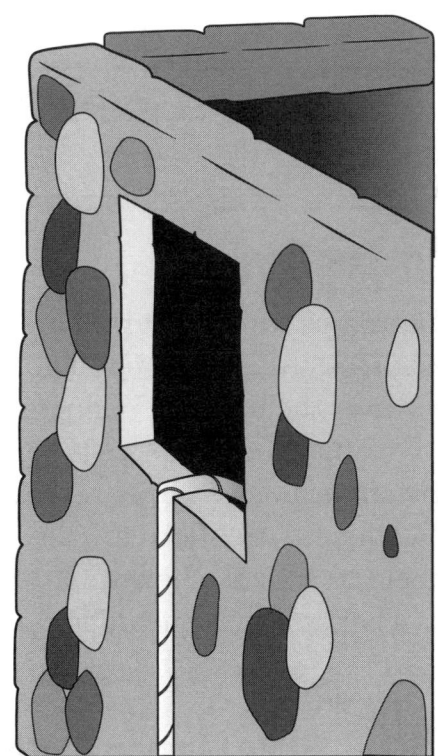

Bible Memory Verse

I will show you my faith by what I do (James 2:18).

Dear Parents and Guardians,

Please check off the items your child completed this week:

- ❑ Prayer Challenge
- ❑ Memory Verse
- ❑ Rahab Trading Card
- ❑ Think and Do

Adult Signature: _____

FAST TRACK! TICKET

And the Winner Is...

Trading Cards

Draw a picture of yourself on the trading card. Add some color and write at the bottom: Winners know that the real prize is being rich in character. Now you have a complete set of cards! Take them to class to show your teacher and the other kids.

Bible Memory Verse

Those who hope in the LORD will renew their strength. They will soar on wings like eagles; they will run and not grow weary, they will walk and not be faint **(Isaiah 40:31)**.

*Early elementary verse in **bold** type.*

Letter Puzzle

Solve the clues and move the numbered letters to the spaces at the bottom of the page to find out what counts in the race of life.

1. Winners 👂 _ _ _ _ _ _ to God.
   <u>1</u>

2. Winners pay attention to God's 👂 _ _ _ _ _ _.
   <u>2</u>

3. Winners choose to give their best in the 👟 _ _ _ of life.
   <u>3</u>

4. Winners 🖼 _ _ _ like winners in all they do.
   <u>4</u>

5. Winners say yes to God's 🔦 _ _ _ _ _ _ _.
   <u>5</u> <u>6</u>

6. Winners 🌳 _ _ _ _ for those around them.
   <u>7</u>

7. Winners choose to be 🦅 _ _ _ _ _ _.
   <u>8</u>

8. Winners 🌍 _ _ _ _ _ God.
   <u>9</u>

WHAT COUNTS?

___ ___ ___ ___ ___ ___ ___ ___ ___
7   6   3   8   5   4   1   2   9

Prayer Challenge

It's hard to always want what God wants for us. But it's the only way to become a winner. Each day as you pray, tell God you want to be a winner, and win the prize he has for you in heaven. Then be silent for a minute so he can direct you as he chooses.

Dear Parents and Guardians,

Please check off the items your child completed this week:

❑ Prayer Challenge
❑ Memory Verse
❑ Yourself Trading Card
❑ Letter Puzzle

Adult Signature:

_____

FAST TRACK! TICKET